CW01429764

Intro to Marketing Automation
Maximize your Advertising ROI

©2015 Todd Kelsey
Contact: tekelsey@gmail.com

TABLE OF CONTENTS

A Note from the Author..6
Chapter Overview 7
   Audience 7
   Features/Scope 7
Chapter 1: What the Heck is Marketing Automation? 9
   Introduction...9
   Understanding Marketing Automation 9
      Fast Forward to Marketing Automation.............................11
      Anonymous Automation 13
   It's All in the Follow-Up: Conversion and Automation 14
      Basic Moving Parts of a Simple Marketing Ecosystem......14
      2B or Not 2B: Traditional CRM and the advent of B2C CRM ...16
   Funnels and Leads: the Terminology of Marketing Automation.....17
      Funnels...17
      Leads 18
      Marketing Automation Poster Child: Lead Nurturing 20
   Industry Perspective: Industry-specific vs General Marketing Automation/CRM
....22
   Conclusion/Discussion..24
   Learning More 24
      For More Information 25
Chapter 2: Tools of the Trade - MailChimp 26
   Introduction...26
   Mailchimp – Email plus Automation......................................26
      Mailchimp In a Nutshell..28
      MailChimp Features...32
      Mailchimp Automation 34
   Conclusion/Discussion..39
   Learning More 40
      Mailchimp 40
      For More Information 40
Chapter 3: Tools of the Trade – Infusionsoft and HubSpot.........41
   Introduction...41
   Infusionsoft 41
      Taking a Closer Look – Infusionsoft 42
   HubSpot 47
      HubSpot Academy 50
      HubSpot Pricing/Features 55
   Note: Sales and Marketing..55
   Industry Perspective: Tools of the Trade 56
   Conclusion/Discussion..58
   Learning More 58

Infusionsoft 58
HubSpot...59
For More Information 59
Chapter 4: Hands On – Make a Free Web Site/Blog............................60
Introduction..60
Create a Google Account/Gmail address..61
Create a Free Website with Google Sites 61
Blogs vs Websites 61
Creating a Site 63
Other Low-Cost/Free Systems 66
Create a Blog..67
Making the Blog...68
Industry Perspective: Web Site Platforms 72
Conclusion/Discussion...76
Learning More 78
Google Sites 78
Other Systems 78
For More Information 78
Chapter 5: Hands On – Starting an Email List 79
Introduction..79
Starting an Account..79
Activation/Configuration 80
Starting a List...84
Get Back to Where You Once Belong 87
See your Email List in Action..87
Looking Ahead..92
Industry Perspective: Email and CRM Systems 93
Conclusion/Discussion...97
Learning More 97
For More Information 97
Chapter 6: Hands On - Collecting Contact Info on Your Blog or Site....98
Introduction..98
Adding a Contact form to a Blog (Blogger) 98
Go into MailChimp to Get the List 99
Get the List into Blogger...101
Adding an email list to a Website (Google Sites)............................105
Industry Perspective: In the Trenches on Social Media...................111
Conclusion/Discussion...112
Learning More 113
For More Information 113
Chapter 7: Hands-On Automating Customer Follow-Up....................114
Introduction..114
A General Suggestion 114
Diving In - Setup..115
Trigger...119
Emails..120

Templates 122
Jedi Powers in Mailchimp...127
Getting Help 130
Exploring Segments – VIPs 131
NOTE: Regarding Mailchimp Free vs Automation....................................133
Exploring Additional Tools 135
Conclusion/Discussion...136
Learning More 136
For More Information 137
Chapter 8: Lead Nurturing with Infusionsoft 138
Introduction...138
Infusionsoft Campaign Builder..138
Creating a New Lead Sequence 142
Delivery Sequence 150
Download Goal 152
Tag Switching 154
Sequence Summary...155
Conclusion/Discussion...155
Learning More 156
For More Information 158
Chapter 9: Lead Nurturing with HubSpot 159
Introduction...159
Getting Help 159
Free Training...160
Starting a Trial 162
Wordpress / HubSpot..168
Finish Configuring HubSpot 172
Getting Started With HubSpot 174
Creating a Landing Page...174
Making Your Own Landing Page 176
Using the Example Landing Page 183
HubSpot Dashboard..184
HubSpot Workflows 186
Congratulations on making it through the hands-on portion of the chapter.
Now on to some Industry Perspective! 191
Industry Perspective: My HubSpot Experience 192
Conclusion/Discussion...195
Learning More 195
For More Information 196
Chapter 10: Going Beyond Google Ads 197
Introduction...197
A Plumber That's Crushing It...197
PPC with No Follow-Up: A Gap to Fill..201
Lifecycle Marketing..204
Industry Perspective: Managing Adwords..209
Conclusion/Discussion...212

For More Information 212
Chapter 11: Case Study – Brian Young of Home Painters Toronto 213
Conclusion/Discussion 220
For More Information 221

A Note from the Author

Before you start reading the book, I invite you to take a look at this short, 2.5 min version of a story that captures the spirit of what's possible with marketing automation: http://tinyurl.com/byoungvid or https://infusionsoft.wistia.com/medias/62oi9vaeeh

Brian Young, Home Painters Toronto

Of all the material I have read and encountered on marketing automation, I found Brian Young's story the most compelling. It actually helped inspire me to write this book, and to learn more about marketing automation myself. One of the simple reasons came down to how he talked about what really matters: in the end, it allowed him to spend more time with his family. It's not magic; it took work to get there, but it was rewarding in the end.

The video is available at: http://tinyurl.com/byoungvid or https://infusionsoft.wistia.com/medias/62oi9vaeeh

There's also an interview and more info in Chapter 11.

Chapter Overview

The goal of the book is to allow the reader to progressively explore marketing automation at your own pace, so you can develop a good understanding and get a sense of related concepts and issues. The book contains helpful explanations in easy to understand language, hands on exercises, and real world perspective.

Audience
- Anyone interested in learning more about marketing automation
- Small to medium size business owners who are ready to take their business to the next level
- Local Service Providers (ex: lawyers, accountants, home improvement contractors)

Features/Scope
- Overview of affordable tools: Mailchimp, Infusionsoft, HubSpot
- Hands-on tour through all the pieces of a basic marketing ecosystem
- Interviews with industry perspective on a variety of related topics

Ch1 - Intro: What the Heck is Marketing Automation? - General intro to marketing automation, high-level view of what an automated marketing campaigns look like, discussion of some of the basic "moving parts" of a simple marketing ecosystem: website, email list, ads, CRM.

Ch2 - Tools of the Trade – Mailchimp - An introduction to MailChimp, a popular email list tool, and discussion of how gathering and managing contact information is the foundation for marketing automation.

Ch3 - Tools of the Trade - Hubspot, Infusionsoft - Overview of two leading marketing automation tools, discussion of the concept of inbound marketing.

Ch4 - Hands-On: Making a Basic Website - Opportunity to try making a website and blog, as a hands-on experience to help understand the basic building blocks of a simple marketing strategy.

Ch5 - Hands-On: Starting an Email List - Opportunity to try creating an email list, using MailChimp.

Ch6 - Hands On: Collecting Contact Info on Your Blog or Site - An exercise in putting some of the pieces together, such as adding a contact form to a blog, and discussion of the role of capturing customer information as part of marketing automation.

Ch7 - Hands-On: Automating Customer Follow-Up - B2C - Step by step exploration of basic automation, to help you understand the basics, using MailChimp.

Ch8 - Lead Nurturing with Infusionsoft - A closer look at how the popular tool Infusionsoft is used for marketing automation.

Ch9 - Lead Nurturing with Hubspot - A closer look at Hubspot, another leading tool.

Ch10 - Going Beyond Google Ads - Industry perspective from Bill Crawford, founder of Rainmaker Internet Marketing. Includes strategies for going beyond pay per click and getting the most out of your ad budget.

Ch11 - Case Study – Brian Young of Home Painters Toronto - An excellent example of how a dedicated approach to marketing automation can transform your business and your life. Pros and cons, challenges, etc.

Chapter 1: What the Heck is Marketing Automation?

Introduction

Welcome!

In this chapter, we'll be taking a closer look at what Marketing Automation is, including how it can help maximize return on investment for a business or organization. Because a business usually has several moving parts in their marketing efforts, we'll look at a "simple marketing ecosystem", to see how the parts work together. This will help provide a foundation for how marketing automation can help things work better, more efficiently.

When you're reading this book, if you're ready to take things to the next level, you're also welcome to schedule a free consultation, to see how Rainmaker Internet Marketing can help your business make use of marketing automation. Please visit rainma.com/automation

Understanding Marketing Automation

My Story: As with other aspects of digital marketing, personally when I first encountered them, I was intimidated. I worked for businesses, had some exposure to the "marketing department", and it seemed like they were lofty wizards who knew arcane techniques. I knew that marketing was necessary for businesses, but I basically dismissed it as being "beyond me".

At some point along the way, I ended up trying to make an ad on Facebook, found it was pretty easy, and that it was actually kind of fun. The fun helped me to forget that I was intimidated by digital marketing, and helped push me through some of the hoops.

In some ways, a simple Facebook ad can help you understand digital marketing, and marketing automation.

A Sunflower Club

Open club where kids of all ages grow monster sunflowers, share seeds and add to a family tree of sunflowers. No green thumb required.

So if you think about it, when you are running an advertisement, you're trying to sell a product or value proposition, and there are a few pieces to the puzzle that you end up working with.

- Content: when you make an ad, you develop content for it, such as ad "copy", images, and other material.
- Ad: when you place the content into the ad itself, you use some set of tools, and a platform. For example, you might put the ad on Facebook.
- Analysis: after you put an ad out there, you'll want to know how it's performing. You might analyze how many people clicked on it, for example.

When I made my first Facebook ad, I didn't know any of these things – I just tried it. But it was fun – putting the text and image together, launching the ad – and it was also fun to see how it performed. The top reason people actually go on Facebook is not to see other peoples' posts, but to see how their own are doing (ex: how many people "liked" a post) – and the same principles apply in digital marketing.

When I started learning about digital marketing, I also didn't realize I was working with an "ecosystem", or that there were a number of moving parts. I just knew that I used Photoshop or Snagit to work with the images – I probably composed the text in Microsoft Word, and then I logged onto Facebook to make it happen.

Fast Forward to Marketing Automation

So when I started hearing about marketing automation, my reaction was similar. I already had some experience with digital marketing, but marketing automation seemed complex. My first taste of it was that a highly enthusiastic owner of a business (my boss at the time), saw great potential in marketing automation to be competitive. They showed me the system, extolled its virtues, and spoke glowingly of all that the system could do – but my eyes glazed over a bit, partly because I didn't really have context. Also the interface of the software seemed clunky as well.

Suffice to say that it wasn't a great experience – but I still realized that marketing automation made sense to consider, and gradually I gained "context", understanding the areas that marketing automation was helping with.

Based on what I know now, I might choose to summarize marketing automation as a simple statement:

Contact the customer, and follow-up with them.
or:

Customer contact and follow-up

If you're a business owner already, then you probably have some history of doing this already, whether you are selling a service or an individual product. And you may be doing some of these things manually, one way or the other, and you may be able to benefit from marketing automation.

And if you boil it all down, regardless of the particular type of business you have, or the type of marketing strategy you have, marketing automation can be thought of as contact and follow-up.

So we can go back to our simple Facebook ad as an example:

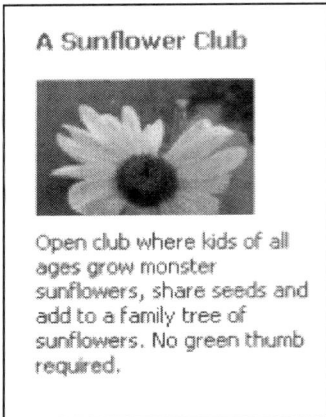

A Sunflower Club

Open club where kids of all ages grow monster sunflowers, share seeds and add to a family tree of sunflowers. No green thumb required.

In this case, I wasn't selling anything per se, just advertising a club people could join – but the audience were customers. And when you're learning about marketing automation, or thinking how it can apply to an organization or business, you can ask the question: how are customers contacted, and how do you follow up with them?

In this case, potential customers are contacted through a Facebook ad, and there wasn't really any follow up – people signed up for the club, or didn't. It was a simple ecosystem.

But what if I did want to follow up with customers? What if I was actually selling something? How would I keep track of people, and how would I follow up with them?

These are the kinds of questions you ask yourself when you're thinking about marketing automation, and the more people you deal with, the more likely you'd benefit from some kind of automation.

Anonymous Automation

One example of marketing automation that may be familiar ⌐ ⌐, is the experience of visiting a website, and then being "followed around" the Internet by ads.

For example, recently I signed up for a service called Relay Rides, to rent out a Tesla. And recently, on many of the news sites I visit, I often see an ad like this, trying to get my attention:

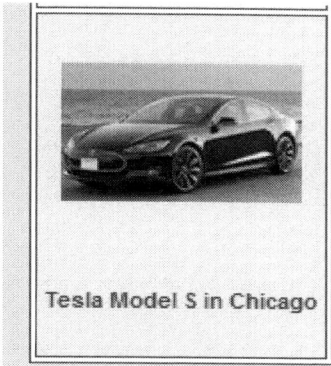

Tesla Model S in Chicago

Technically this is known as "display retargeting", and its anonymous, based on cookies. To unpack that a bit, when you visit a website, you may be "cookied" (ex: like going to a concert or bar and getting a stamp on your hand). It's a file that gets created in your Internet browser, and a company can choose to have an ad campaign that displays ads to people who have visited their website.

It's a simple example of automated follow up – someone visits your site, and you don't have their contact information, but in some cases, when visiting other websites, they may see your ad, and it's a reminder.

It's All in the Follow-Up: Conversion and Automation

What happens in most businesses and organizations, especially when there's a website and digital marketing involved, is that you end up with a lot of lost opportunities. For example, people may visit your site, but they might not "convert", that is, they might not purchase a product or request more information.

And typically, the more people you are talking about, the harder it is to follow up individually with potential customers, so the more manual your process is for following up, the more opportunities are lost.

So the basic value of a marketing automation, in general, is that it can help automate follow-up, and allow you to keep track of customers more efficiently and easily.

Basic Moving Parts of a Simple Marketing Ecosystem

In order to understand the role of marketing automation systems, it's helpful to consider the typical "ecosystem" that a business often has. The exact parts vary significantly from business to business, but it's at least representative. For example, you might have a business that sells a product, and when you are able to get their contact information, email can be used to contact them with the goal of visiting the website again.

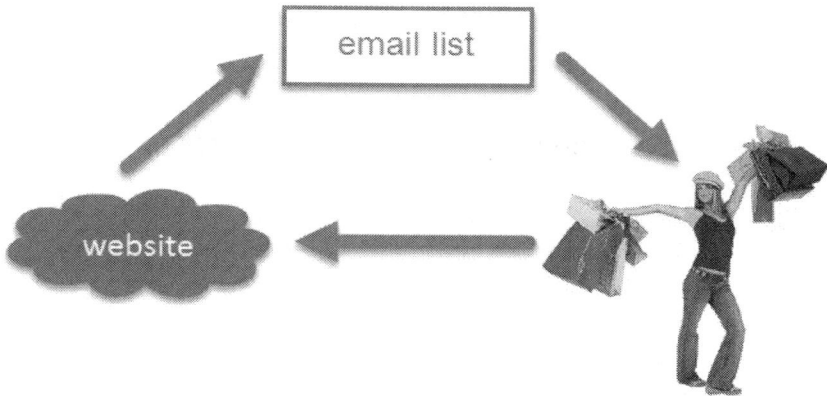

That doesn't sound too bad – but what if you forget to email people? Or what if you want to split up your customers into different groups, and send different emails? What if some people call in?

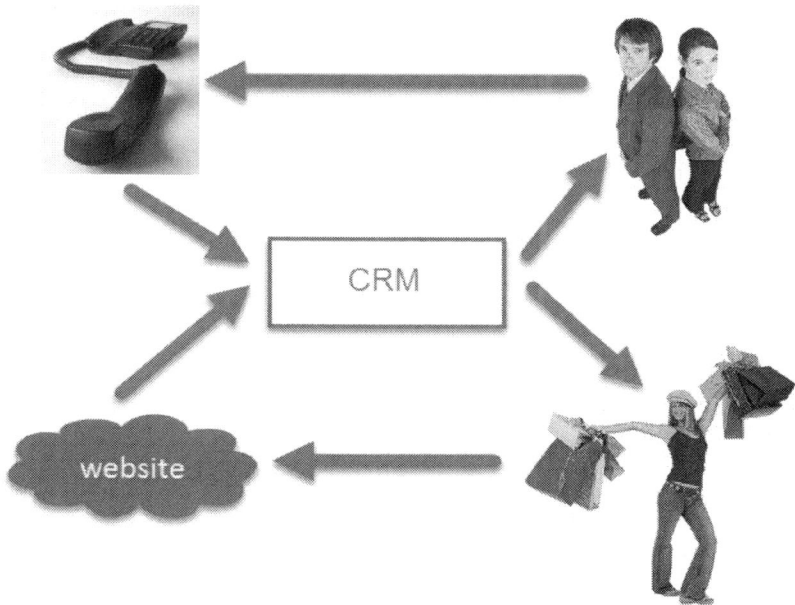

At some point in the misty past, CRM (Customer Relationship Management) systems began to arise, to help people keep track of this kind of information, to help manage the process of customer follow-up.

CRM systems often grew out of email systems – makes sense, right? If you have to keep track of a bunch of email addresses, why not keep contact information all in one place?

2B or Not 2B: Traditional CRM and the advent of B2C CRM

If you are a business owner you may already know this, but generally businesses and organizations will fall into one of two categories: B2C (business to consumer), or B2B (business to business).

In general, historically the most likely business to adopt a system to help manage customers would be in the B2B category, such as a company providing services or products to other businesses. In many cases, the profile of a typical CRM system would be that it is used by a sales force – that is, where there is actually a need for salespeople to follow up with potential customers on a one to one basis.

As technology has progressed, marketing automation has also been increasingly used in B2C (business to consumer) settings – that is, where there's not necessarily a salesperson following up.

For some businesses, this is the holy grail – where you have a customer, or potential customer, and as much as possible is automated, so that you use as little internal resources as possible, to control your costs, and become more profitable. This principle of efficiency and automation applies to both B2B and B2C – and it's a matter of the lost opportunities mentioned earlier. Not only can marketing automation help you more efficiently deal with more people, but it can also help to act upon opportunities that otherwise are lost.

Another way of saying it is, marketing automation can result in more sophisticated marketing, and if the right pieces are in place, and there's a strategy, it can definitely have a positive impact on your business.

One of the values of learning about the various moving pieces is that it can help you answer some of the basic questions that may come up when you are thinking of these things:

- what system do I need?
- can I connected a new system to something I am already using?
- how do I strike a balance between capability, and cost?

It's a good idea to get an understanding of the basics, so that you can think critically about the various options. For example, marketing automation is a "hot phrase", and any number of businesses, software companies and consultants may say "we can do marketing automation" or "our system does marketing automation", but the most important question to ask is, *to what extent* can a system do marketing automation, and even more importantly, *what does my business need*. What will be the return on investment?

Funnels and Leads: the Terminology of Marketing Automation

In digital marketing and marketing automation, there's a lot of terms and acronyms floating about, but there are two concepts that are helpful to understand, which provide a context for developing strategy, and understanding the capability of related systems.

Funnels

The first time I heard this marketing term, I was like, what? Funnel cakes? Like the kind I used to buy at a carnival when I was a kid? Nope, this is a different kind of funnel.

It's like the kind where you would want to direct something (ex: when you're adding oil to a car engine) – wide at the top, narrow at the bottom.

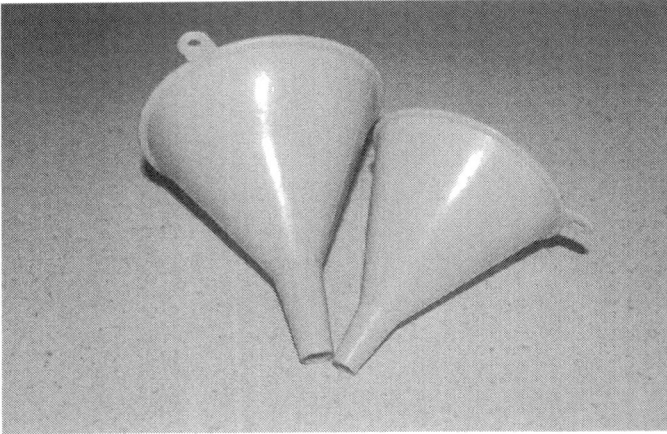

As part of overall marketing strategy, many businesses think of customers and potential customers in terms of funnels. Basically at the top of the funnel, you have everyone who is aware of your business, product, who sees an ad, or who visits one of your locations, or your website. The funnel is wide at the top. And gradually, through various techniques, your goal is to "draw people further into the funnel", and "convert" them into paying customers.

Leads

A lead is another term that's closely tied to marketing automation, and the tradition of sales. The term lead is also interchangeable with sales lead. Basically, salespeople are always looking for leads – that is, people who might be interested in learning more about a product or service.

If you think of our funnel, you can consider how potential customers, or "leads" are at the top, and gradually the pool is narrowed down into those who actually become customers.

So you might have a website that makes products available, and use advertisements to "Drive" people to your website. By doing this, you're placing them in the funnel. You could also say that advertisements themselves are at the very top of the funnel.

But if we go back to our original example of an email list, the more *passive* a business is, the more lost opportunities there are. For example, using the above technique, you may very well generate sales – ads lead people to the site who purchase the product. But if you make no attempt to gather peoples' contact information, then you're missing out on the opportunity to follow up.

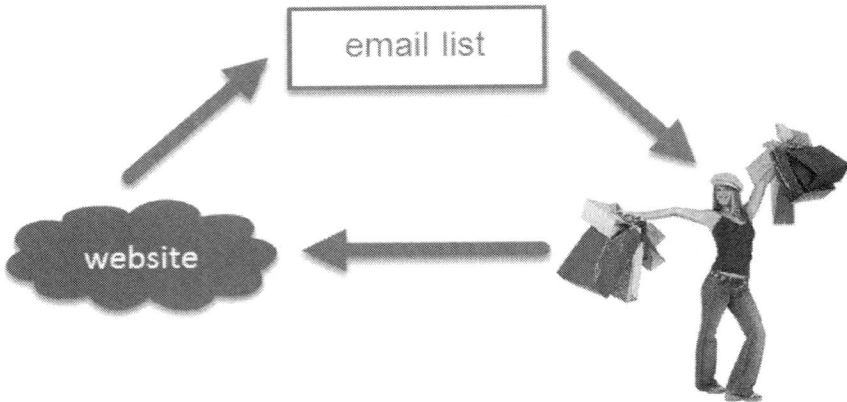

And if you think about all the people who visit your website, and don't purchase a product – that's another significant lost opportunity. There may be people who are interested, open, but it's not the right time. Or they need to learn more before they make a decision. If you never make an effort to *generate* and *nurture* leads, then it's a lost opportunity. And very likely, you will lose those potential customers to the competition.

Marketing Automation Poster Child: Lead Nurturing

Lead nurturing is one of the prime examples of where marketing automation can help a business, whether it's B2C, B2B or something else.

Here's a behind the scenes look at Infusionsoft, one of the popular tools we'll be looking at. This is a view of the "campaign builder", for what is known as a lead nurturing sequence.

| Start | Run on 1-1-2016 at 8:00 AM | Thank Clients | Run on 1-8-2016 at 8:00 AM | Call Clients |

In this case, a business owner wants to maintain a good relationship with current clients, and hopefully earn their repeat business. This sequence of events generates an email thanking clients for their business, and then waits a week, and then notifies an employee to make a follow up call to see how they're doing.

Not that big of a deal, right? You could send an email a week after they purchase something, then call them a week later. But what if the number of customers grows, and people buy at different times? To even do a very simple amount of customer follow up can be a complex task, but it's also something that can be automated.

In this case, it's "semi-automated", because there's a reminder for an employee to actually call people. But you could just as easily have a fully-automated sequence, which is increasingly popular with ecommerce businesses, which basically amounts to being a series of follow up emails.

As you can imagine, different types of businesses have different needs for attracting and nurturing leads, and as a result, a variety of options exist, including systems that have been customized for a particular sector (ex: real estate), vs systems that can be applied to any industry. We'll now turn to Bill Crawford, principal at Rainmaker Internet Marketing, for some perspective, as we explore this area.

Industry Perspective: Industry-specific vs General Marketing Automation/CRM

Bill Crawford,
Founder and President of
Rainmaker Internet Marketing

Todd: What have you noticed about the rise of industry-specific software (CRM/marketing automation) vs generic systems?

Bill: A lot of industry specific software arose out of a particular industry - they had no intention initially of going to market, they just wanted an efficient in-house tool. Then peers would come along, notice how it was helping their business, and say "Hey, can I have access to that tool?" For example, Improveit 360 is an example of a software platform for the home improvement industry, which was later acquired by Salesforce.

One of my own mentors advised me to evaluate software based on asking, does it have workflow strengths or sales and marketing strengths? Because often software will fall into those categories. Another way of saying "workflow strengths" would be productivity, where, the software is good at helping you manage a business from an efficiency standpoint. But other software might be stronger at helping you with sales/marketing.

In terms of marketing automation/CRM software, what I've seen is that Industry-specific software speaks to the industry, has a customized workflow, usually very content rich. Someone's already thought through ways of speaking to a customer for that industry. And industry-specific software seems to have more of an internal/workflow emphasis. The creators have sought internal efficiency, perhaps good reporting capabilities, content rich. It can give a manager good visibility about where things are at internally, where a customer might be in various stages in sales, sold not installed, etc.

But some of the general, customizable platforms like Infusionsoft can have more of a sales/marketing strength, but still be applied effectively to various industries. For example, after you capture your customer information, you could have more options for a customized campaign to capture and nurture leads. A general platform gives you a lot of options, for scheduling, timing, and experimenting. The customizability may help you test the most effective strategy.

Another thing I've seen is that sometimes industry-specific tools might say "we have automation". But you have to look carefully at the *extent* of the automation, how much it can be customized and adapted to your needs, to give you the most leads. For example, "limited" automation might be a simple limited scenario, where a customer calls, and you can click on a button, to automatically send them a thank you for contacting your company. That's it.

Or if the customer books a time and a date, there's a button to send email: "thank you for scheduling". A limited platform may be *calling* it automation. But the problem might be, the software might be forcing everyone to do workflow with a one size fits all approach. So you have to ask yourself, do you want to structure your company around software?

One of the problems with this is that people are resistant to change. One significant reason new tools can fail is from lack of adoption. For example, one of the top reasons CRM initiatives fail at a company is lack of adoption. Someone finds a great tool but no one uses it. So customizability can be important, because it can make it easier to adapt to what people are used to, and also give them an opportunity to have input into the process.

So to me, the capabilities of general tools seem far superior. You can customize the workflow, and optimize things to have a greater impact on generating leads, such as figuring out the best sequence for follow-up, and having it as automated as possible.

Conclusion/Discussion

Congratulations on making it through this first chapter! You've gotten some exposure to basic principles and concepts, and this will help you to get more out of the next chapter, where we'll take a look at some of the popular "tools of the trade", including Infusionsoft, and HubSpot.

Don't be discouraged if you're not "Getting it" yet – my general recommendation is to think of the chapters in this book like coats of paint. Read the first section to get a sense of the high-level concepts, and then in Section 2, we'll dive in with some hands on practice, which will help make things more concrete.

If you're ready to take things to the next level, you're also welcome to schedule a free consultation, to see how Rainmaker Internet Marketing can help your business make use of marketing automation. Please visit rainma.com/automation

Learning More

Here's some links to get you started.

Infusionsoft Review - #1 Small Business CRM & Marketing Automation Software
https://www.youtube.com/watch?v=YmdjBrhY2dA
> A short video that describes Infusionsoft capabilities and helps you get a sense of what marketing automation can be used to do.

Small Business Sales CRM and Email Marketing Automation Software - InTouch
https://www.youtube.com/watch?v=0tywe5tvGFs
> An even shorter video, that gets across some of the concepts, from a different system.

Why Marketing Automation Software Fails to Deliver
https://www.youtube.com/watch?v=w9DArlMxzS8

> This is a slightly longer video (10 minutes), where there's some good discussion of things to keep in mind when considering marketing automation. It's "pro marketing automation", but demonstrates that a strategy is necessary to help make use of the system. The equivalent of the video can also be seen at this blog post: http://www.crmsearch.com/why-marketing-software-fails.php

For More Information

For a complete list of links and resources, visit rainma.com/book

Chapter 2: Tools of the Trade - MailChimp

Introduction

In this chapter, we'll be taking a closer look at MailChimp, a leading email platform, which is easy to use, and has a free version that you can try to get used to the program. Mailchimp also has some automation capability, which requires an upgrade, but it's relatively inexpensive (at the present time, $10 USD/month). So Mailchimp can be a way to try some basic marketing automation out.

When you're reading this book, if you're ready to take things to the next level, you're also welcome to schedule a free consultation, to see how Rainmaker Internet Marketing can help your business make use of marketing automation. Please visit rainma.com/automation

Mailchimp – Email plus Automation

Mailchimp is a leading email management tool, and email management is an important part of the marketing automation "ecosystem", so it's a good thing to consider. But don't worry if you've never had an email list before. I didn't either! Until very recently.

I would fall into the category of having been exposed to email marketing in various settings, including a popular platform Constant Contact – but personally, I'd never really run an email list. I've had personal projects, website, etc. – but the hassle and cost of setting up email always seemed too much. And up until recent years, setting up an email list and sending emails seemed to require technical maintenance and upkeep, and I didn't want to deal with that.

Fast forward to recent times, and for some odd reason, I had actually dismissed email, didn't even consider it, when I started working on a project called NPOEx. I created a website, and as part of raising awareness, I dutifully tried out social media marketing, thinking that making a Facebook page and getting as many likes I could would be the best way to get a following and then be able to communicate with them.

I was in the startup mentality, and after learning more about Kickstarter, applying to startup accelerators, etc. – I kept coming across the principle of needing to develop a following before you bring things to the next level, and gradually I realized (duh!) that I needed to return to the basics: making an email list.

Partly my expectations were based on the way that Facebook used to work, before they started changing algorithms and that communication with your followers became more difficult, and less clear, than email. As for me, I invested in some Facebook ads, got some people to like the Facebook page at http://facebook.com/npoex - but then gradually realized that even though I had 1,000 likes, not very many people were even seeing the posts, for one reason or another. And when I started trying to send Facebook messages to individual people (to whom I had paid Facebook originally to send an advertisement), I found that Facebook didn't like me sending individual messages to that many people. So I got a bit frustrated and annoyed with Facebook. Yes, social media is an important thing to consider, but it's a good example of thinking critically about ROI (return on investment), and making sure that no matter what things you try, that you have a central database of contact information for your customers, which *you* control.

So if you're in the category of asking yourself – where do I begin? I'd actually invite you to consider beginning with a website, of course – but then proceeding directly to starting an email list – even if you switch to a different tool later. Developing the mindset of being concerned less about tools, and more about the customer relationship and information, can help you feel the freedom to take your data into whatever system works best for you.

So, for learning some of the basics, in Chapter 5, we'll go hands-on and create a live email campaign in Mailchimp. But in the following segments, there's an overview of Mailchimp in a nutshell and then a closer look at some of the automation it can do.

Mailchimp In a Nutshell

Here's a simple behind the scenes look at a real world Mailchimp example. Without getting too fancy, I used Mailchimp to make a basic template, entered some of the basic information, and have used it a number of times. It's relatively easy to use, has a friendly interface, and is actually fun.

Below we see a preview of a recent email I sent out.

And one of the things to understand about email systems is that they're not just keeping track of the email addresses for you, but they help to automate the process of collecting the information in the first place, and some of the hoops that you have to jump through when managing an email list.

So it used to be that in order to gather any customer information, you'd have to manually create a form on a web page, and then send it somewhere. In some cases it may have just in turn sent you an email with a new email address to add to you contact book, spreadsheet, etc. – there's nothing wrong with that per se, but it can be time-consuming, and there's reasons to make use of the latest technology.

So if we return to my research project, I basically wanted to get a decent website going with a minimum of time required, without having to hire a designer or web developer. So I ended up using Strikingly (www.strikingly.com), and when I started the free Mailchimp account, it was as easy as adding a link to one of the sections on the Strikingly site (http://npoex.com).

And when you click on the link, it leads to a page that Mailchimp automatically created for me, that asks for people's information.

So while you might be tempted to just "manually" take peoples' email addresses, it's really better to have an email management tool – partly because it automates some of the important things that are good to do these days, such as getting a confirmation that someone really wants to be on the list, by emailing one out and asking people to click on the link:

NPOEx Newsletter

Almost finished...

We need to confirm your email address.

To complete the subscription process, please click the link in the email we just sent you.

NPOEx
P.O. Box 1302
Wheaton, IL 60187

Add us to your address book

« return to our website

To do things right on a basic level, there are a lot of moving pieces, even with email, and that's where a free tool like Mailchimp can come in really handy, even if you are doing a small project on the side.

One of the most important bases to have covered is compliance with the CAN-SPAM act, which specifies the kinds of things you need to have in place in order not to be in the grey area of spamming people. You really need to communicate clearly, including having a way for people to unsubscribe, easily (i.e. not relying on you to manually take someone off of a list), and also having clearly identifiable contact information, etc.

And systems like Mailchimp take care of that. There are templates available, and forms you fill out to get the basic information in place.

Below is an example of the email "footer" that mailchimp automatically generates, to help manage things like unsubscribing from an email list.

Thanks again for your interest, and please let me know if you have any questions.

Carpe diem!

- Dr. Todd Kelsey, PhD

MailChimp Features

Here's a look at some features of Mailchimp; there are distinctives but it's fairly representative of some of the other email tools out there, and to one extent or another, they're all responding to the increased interest in marketing automation and often building automation onto the email platform, such as the way Mailchimp is.

I recommend taking a look at: http://mailchimp.com/features/

And reading up on the site about their automation features – this is a little wonky, but a sample of the language of automation.

Automation and personalization

MailChimp helps you email the right people at the right time. Send automated emails based on customer behavior and preferences. Get started with pre-built Workflows or use our built-in segmentation and targeting options to build custom rules. And get in-depth reporting on how each of your automated series is performing. Our tools help you learn more about your customers and send them timely, relevant content.

You'll also want to take a look at their automation section:

http://mailchimp.com/features/automation/

You can see some of the capabilities. In some cases, in order to automate some things, you end up having to make technical connections between your website, or shopping cart, or both – and that's where integration may come in.

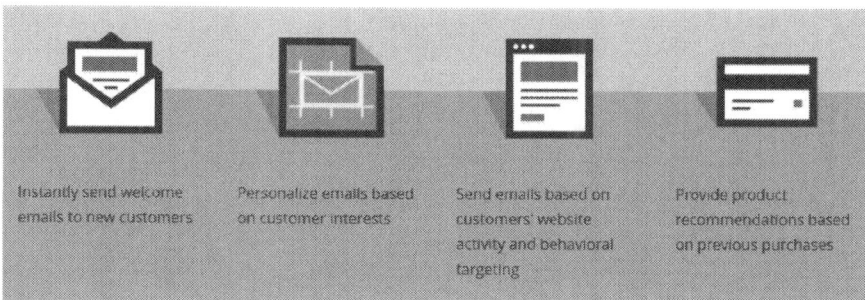

Instantly send welcome emails to new customers

Personalize emails based on customer interests

Send emails based on customers' website activity and behavioral targeting

Provide product recommendations based on previous purchases

For example, you might start an ecommerce site on the Shopify.com platform, and then integrate it with Mailchimp, so that when someone purchases something, you've got their contact information in your database, you're starting to get a sense of their interests, and Mailchimp would be able to send out emails to thank customers for their business and to present new offers.

Then at some point you might be interested in more advanced automation, which Mailchimp refers to as workflow.

Control your workflow

Workflows let you control the conditions for your automated emails. View all of your messages in one place, and drag-and-drop to determine their send order.

Mailchimp Automation

In the paid version of MailChimp, you can log in and create an automation workflow.

Automation

Create Automation Workflow

You have no automation workflows

Automatically send one-to-one emails to subscribers to improve e-commerce sales, educate customers, and more.

You select an email list to work with:

Which list do you want to use?

Select a list to see workflows.

Select A List ⌄

Then there are a number of pre-built workflows that you can customize, depending on what you want to do.

Welcome Message
Send a welcome email after a subscriber joins your list.

Select

Educate Subscribers
Send a series of emails, like a getting started guide or online course, when subscribers join your list.

Select

Welcome Series
Send a series of onboarding emails when subscribers join your list.

Select

API 3.0
Send an email when triggered with an API 3.0 call.

Select

Custom
Mix and match triggers, segments, and emails to create a custom workflow.

Selected

Website Activity
Send emails after a subscriber navigates from a campaign to a URL on your site with Goal tracking enabled.
Requires Goal

Using the Welcome series as an example, you enter in basic information to begin with:

Workflow name

Welcome to NPOEx

Internal use only. Ex: "Newsletter Test#4"

From name   95 characters remaining

NPOEx

Use something subscribers will instantly recognize, like your company name.

From email address

tekelsey@gmail.com

☐ **Send activity digest email**
We'll send you an email every day with a report so you can see how this workflow is performing.

☐ **Use Conversations to manage replies**
When enabled, we'll generate a special reply-to address for your email. We'll filter "out of office" replies, then thread conversations into your subscribers' profiles and display them in reports.

☑ **Personalize the "To:" field**
Include the recipient's name in the message using merge tags to make it more personal and help avoid spam filters. For example, *|FNAME|* *|LNAME|* will show "To: Bob Smith" in the email instead of "To: bob@example.com". This is more personal and may help avoid spam filters.

Specify *|MERGETAGS|* for recipient name

|FNAME|

Then, you can configure the "trigger" – that is, what triggers a person to be placed in the sequence for a series of emails.

Configure Trigger

Welcome Series · Change workflow

Trigger workflow when the following conditions are met:

People subscribe to list **NPOEx Newsletter**

☐ **Trigger workflow when subscribers are imported**
Imported subscribers **will not** be added to this workflow

☐ **Add segmentation conditions**

☐ **Send first email immediately to existing subscribers who meet conditions**

On what days should emails be sent?

☑ Sun ☑ Mon ☑ Tue ☑ Wed ☑ Thu ☑ Fri ☑ Sat

Then you can add emails to the workflow, and this is where you get to the nitty gritty of marketing automation. In this case we might call it a "welcome sequence", but another common "Sequence" is a lead nurture sequence. In that case, you are using automation to help follow up with a potential customer.

In this case, you are sending a series of emails to welcome a new customer. It might be that you have mailchimp send an email once a week, or once a month, introducing the new customer to a feature of your website, or sending out some helpful links. The main point, is that such things can be automated.

It doesn't meant that just because you can do x, y and z, with an automation platform, you should do so as much as possible. The idea is to learn the best practices for how often to follow up with people, and under what conditions. An easy starting place would be to consider yourself – would you want to get a follow up email? What kinds of things would you be interested in?

Now add emails to this workflow.

For Welcome Series, we recommend starting with 5 emails.

You can always add more or remove them later.

Add 5 Emails   or   Add 1 Email

You might take Mailchimps suggestion of adding 5 emails as a starting point.

- 2 days after workflow is triggered · Change delay

✎	?	Automation Email #1 Edited on Jun 24, 2015 01:16 pm by you	Design Email	🗑

- 3 days after previous email is sent · Change delay

✎	?	Automation Email #2 Edited on Jun 24, 2015 01:16 pm by you	Design Email	🗑

And this is where you get into sequencing. 2 days after the "workflow is triggered" (in this case, when someone joins the email list), they could get a nice welcome email. Then, three days after that, you could follow up with a popular article related to your product/service/organization. And so on.

The general principle is that to a certain extent, "if" you offer something relevant that people want (ex: new information, offers, insight, deals), and if you don't send it too often, people might actually open it, and the follow-up emails may help to keep people engaged. Not everyone is going to be the same, but you can talk to customers and find out the kind of things they'd appreciate knowing about.

That, in a nutshell, is marketing automation in Mailchimp, and the very basics of marketing automation.

Where does one tool end and another begin? It's hard to say, but it's also safe to say that things are always changing. It would be understandable if you were looking at marketing automation and your eyes started glazing over with all the options – my advice is to think about your business and think about your customers, and actually talk to them. And then come up with an idea of the kind of things you'd like to try, and then start trying them – such as new customer follow-up – or lead nurture, and so on.

When you start getting into it, when you're basing your exploration around your business needs, then you start looking at the options in a different way – they become part of your toolbox. And you might start out by just sending emails out – then you might get curious about the performance of the email campaign, such as how many people clicked on the email. That might lead you to learn more about analytics, and the different kinds of things you can track. So my recommendation, especially if you're just starting out, is to explore things incrementally, including trying a simpler less expensive tool, until you outgrow it.

Conclusion/Discussion

Congratulations on making it through the second chapter and getting to know more about marketing automation!

You've gotten some exposure to email management, an important part of the marketing automation ecosystem, and you've seen how marketing automation is an outgrowth of maintaining the customer relationship, such as through email. In the next chapter, we'll step things up a notch and take a look at two more tools, Infusionsoft and HubSpot, with more powerful automation capabilities.

If you're ready to take things to the next level, you're also welcome to schedule a free consultation, to see how Rainmaker Internet Marketing can help your business make use of marketing automation. Please visit rainma.com/automation

Learning More

Here's some links to get you started.

Mailchimp

www.mailchimp.com

Mailchimp Marketing Automation Workflows
https://www.youtube.com/watch?v=NuftV4sp99M
> video showing some of the workflows in Mailchimp and how they're used for automation.

Mailchimp Tutorial: How To Create A Mailchimp Email Campaign
https://www.youtube.com/watch?v=8SPzGqUJDU0
> 15 minute video that helps you get a sense of how Mailchimp works

How To Use Mailchimp Step By Step Full Tutorial For BEGINNERS (Free Email Marketing)
https://www.youtube.com/watch?v=5KAnqy5YOeI
> Longer video on mailchimp

For More Information

For a complete list of links and resources, visit rainma.com/book

Chapter 3: Tools of the Trade – Infusionsoft and HubSpot

Introduction

In this chapter, we'll be taking a closer look at Infusionsoft and HubSpot, two more popular tools of the trade, with more extensive capability to help you explore marketing automation.

When you're reading this book, if you're ready to take things to the next level, you're also welcome to schedule a free consultation, to see how Rainmaker Internet Marketing can help your business make use of marketing automation. Please visit rainma.com/automation

Infusionsoft

If you thought of Mailchimp as a really fine sailboat that could take you just about anywhere, but with some limitations, then Infusionsoft might be something like a high-performance speedboat – or a battleship, as it were – more flexible, more customizable, and generally more powerful.

Infusionsoft has marketing automation capability, just like the kind Mailchimp has, but it's more flexible and powerful, and there are a number of examples of small to mid-sized businesses that have made a committed effort to using Infusionsoft, and have seen a significant impact on their business, including reducing the time it takes to manage all the moving pieces of "lead generation", as well increasing their revenue, in some cases very significantly. Businesses have gone from being overwhelmed by details, towards growth and having a high-performance, growing operation with more employees.

Taking a Closer Look – Infusionsoft

As you explore marketing automation, I'd recommend visiting this page and taking a look at some of the "success stories" of people who've used Infusionsoft, and the impact that it's had on their business. This can help give you inspiration to dive further in.

http://www.infusionsoft.com/success-stories

CLEANCORP CLEANING SERVICE
A young Australian family finds success through quality service and automation

LEFTFOOT COACHING ACADEMY
Soccer trainer finds space to help young athletes grow.

SALON SUCCESS STRATEGIES
Salon-specific marketing agency gets a brand new look.

ROEDER STUDIOS
Social media consultant grows with Infusionsoft

MINT SOCIAL
Social media marketing agency helps businesses stay fresh

OPTIBIKE
Electric bike maker revs up sales.

Infusionsoft would fall into the "integrated solution" category. As Bill Crawford comments in the Industry Perspective at the end of this chapter, he's seen businesses step back and look at the tools their using, and transition successfully into putting all things under one roof. There are reasons that can be helpful – sometimes integrating tools can be a headache.

But some people may start using Infusionsoft for the automation capability, connect it to their CRM system or their current email tool. This is where the "ecosystem" concept comes in from the first chapter – every business is different, but there are some common pieces.

When you log in to Infusionsoft, the high-level menu gives an idea of the capability of the program.

My Nav	CRM	Marketing	E-Commerce	Admin
Basic Training	Contacts	Campaign Builder	E-Commerce Setup	Branding Center
Initial Setup	Companies	Email & Broadcasts	Orders	Infusionsoft Account
Dashboard	Opportunities	Lead Generation	Products	Users
My Day	Referral Partners	Templates	Actions	Import Data
	Visitors	Legacy	Promotions	Data Cleanup
			Legacy	
Edit	Reports Settings	Reports Settings	Reports Settings	Reports Settings

In the middle, in Marketing, the Campaign Builder is the central automation tool, but a number of businesses make extensive, profitable use of the CRM capabilities, and e-commerce capabilities.

So if we compare Infusionsoft to Mailchimp, there are some similar considerations when automating workflow, but there are a lot more options.

In the Campaign Builder, you basically get a blank canvas for building sequences.

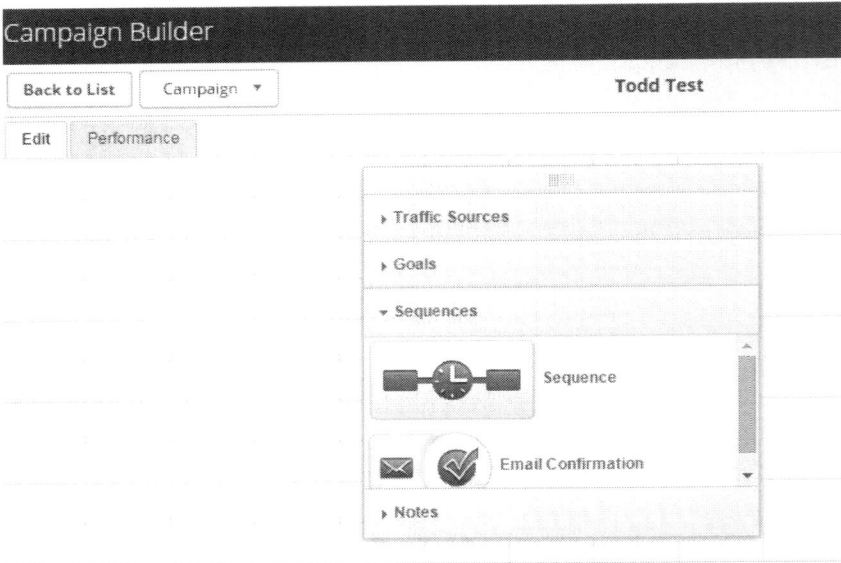

So you drag and drop elements out into the workspace, and then connect them.

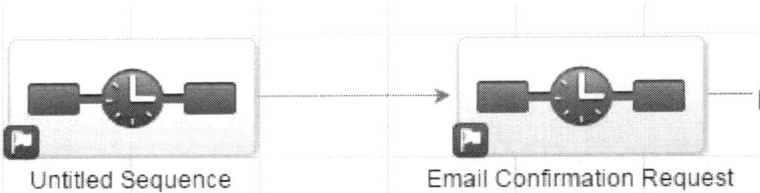

There are also a lot of templates that you can use and customize to your needs.

One way to help understand the possibilities of Infusionsoft and more sophisticated marketing automation, is the way you can customize and experiment.

For example, here's a high-level view of a live automated campaign, which includes nurturing leads.

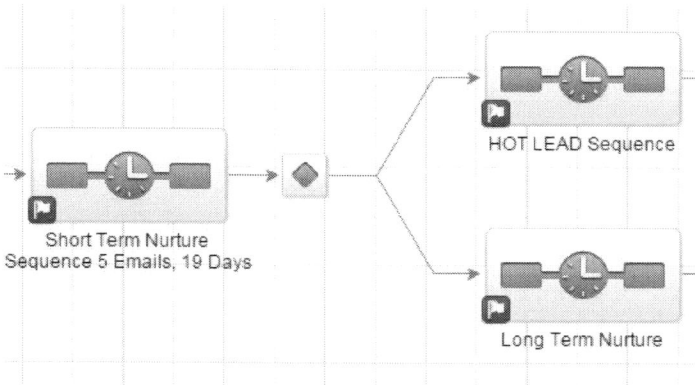

And if we take a closer look at just the short term nurture sequence that was created, you can see the level of detail possible

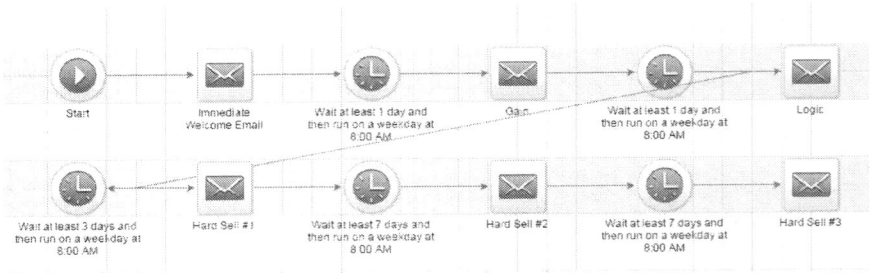

To help decode the above, the overall idea is that when someone downloads the ebook, they're placed in a sequence to "nurture them along". If you feel squeamish, rightly so, about not wanting to spam people, that's a good thing. But remember that these particular people already showed some particular interest.

And there are best practices, industry benchmarks, and guidelines, of the best way to follow up with people, so that you can encourage people who "might" be interested, to explore things a little bit more. There's no universally right way to do it, but being able to customize things helps.

In the above, a series of emails is sent, and initially, the frequency is short, and then it goes to sending emails about weekly. And the way it is designed – if someone acts upon any of the emails, it pulls them out of this sequence, and puts them in another.

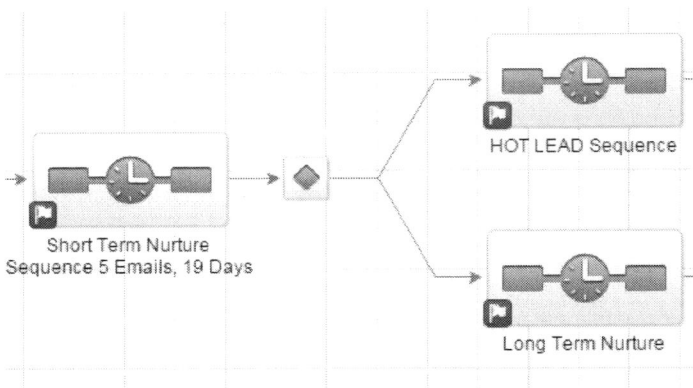

So if the potentially interested person says, "yeah, sure I'd like to schedule a call", they've become a "hot lead", important to follow up on in a different way.

So basically, when you look at your customers, and potential customers, and test out the sequence that works best for your business, the overall "return on investment" is that you are helping to get customers who would otherwise fall through the cracks (Ex: maybe because you didn't remember to email them, or didn't have time, etc.)

Another thing to keep in mind is that marketing automation can automate more than just lead nurturing or follow up emails – systems can be used to notify employees to actually call people, to set a sequence of events in motion based pooling people into different categories (such as stages of research, where different material is needed, etc.). But by following what customers are actually interested in, and by working to provide that information, value, or resource at the right time, you can significantly impact your performance, and automation can help in that process.

HubSpot

HubSpot, like Infusionsoft, is an extensive and highly customizable platform. HubSpot is known as a thought leader in the field of "inbound marketing", which they have championed. As a company, they've been involved extensively in showing many businesses how you can attract customers by placing the right *content* on your site.

To begin, I'd recommend looking at 1 or more of the case studies of people using HubSpot.

http://www.hubspot.com/customers

You can browse case studies:

You can also sort by different business categories, to drill down to a case study that's most relevant to your own business.

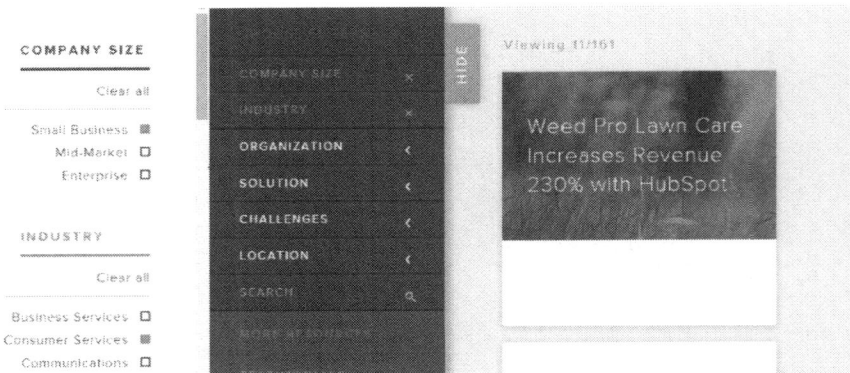

(Above link: http://www.hubspot.com/customers#/f=consumer-services/small-business)

HubSpot's main message is that people are overwhelmed with "outbound" marketing, including advertisements of all kinds. And one of their primary principles is that you need to situate yourself at the right place, at the right time as people are doing research for products or services. So for some businesses, this might involve delivering helpful information about a topic (ex: refrigerator efficiency), in the form of an e-book, for example, and people who are looking for this information might wind up on your site. In this scenario, they didn't come because of an advertisement per se, it's more because of a value proposition – they're looking for information.

HubSpot also has helpful material to demonstrate the importance of not taking a "one size fits all" message with your customers. They advocate creating customer "personas", so that the message you are bringing, and the material you develop, is tailored to the different segments of your potential audience. For example, you might have one message that's perfect for teens, but doesn't strike the same chord with grandparents. This kind of mentality, of basing marketing truly around the customer, can add a lot of power to your marketing efforts.

It's not that you need the HubSpot platform to act on these principles, per se – but HubSpot can rightly claim that their platform is highly optimized for inbound marketing.

Like Infusionsoft, compared to Mailchimp, if Mailchimp is a very capable sailboat or yacht, then HubSpot might be like an aircraft carrier. But when doing comparisons, it's also fair to say that the question of the best platform to use really depends on the business. Some businesses may not need or be able to make use of anything more than the basic automation capability that Mailchimp provides.

This is partly why I recommend exploring things incrementally – exploring a tool like Mailchimp to understand the basics, and thinking of your business model first, and your customers – not the tool per se. And then progressively looking at how a more advanced tool might be able to help strengthen your business.

HubSpot Academy

With HubSpot, one thing I'd say is that their educational material is top notch, and can help you understand the principles of inbound marketing.

I'd strongly recommend visiting HubSpot Academy, watching their free videos, and even going for the certification. It's helpful, but relatively easy. If you prefer reading material, you can also download a PDF study guide or a set of individual powerpoints that come with each lesson.

http://academy.hubspot.com/certification

To repeat, the principles of inbound marketing don't only apply to the HubSpot platform, which is why I highly recommend going through their material, to understand how powerful some of the principles are, in helping to strengthen and grow your business.

We are only looking at a snapshot of all of HubSpot's features here, but like Infusionsoft, there's an overall dashboard, and then a Campaign area alongside the other options.

In HubSpot, you might structure your campaigns to appeal to the different "personas" you've identified. Instead of templates, HubSpot offers pre-defined "recipes" that you can use.

Campaigns   ⊙ Creating a Campaign   ▶ Overview Video   **Create a new campaign**

📅 All campaigns ▾	🌐 By anyone ▾	👤 All personas ▾	🔍 Search campaigns

Campaign Name	Start Date ▾	End Date	🏷 Browse Recipes Explore commonly used campaigns
Marketing Manager, Medium-Sized – Jennifer	2/1/2015	4/30/2015	⚙ ▾
5 Things for Small Business - Sam	11/23/2014	1/31/2015	⚙ ▾
Medium-Sized Business Owner - Mike			⚙ ▾

When you create a new campaign, many of the options are related to content, figuring out the path people might take to be drawn into your "funnel".

Convert Contacts

○	**Keywords** Create New or Associate	Target specific keywords with your campaign so you can get found organically.	Learn more about keywords ✕
○	**Landing Pages** Create New	In this step you can create the landing and thank you pages that will present a platform for your offer	Learn more about landing pages ✕

Promote Campaign

○	**Emails** Create New	Build a marketing email aligned with your landing page so you can promote the offer to your existing contacts.	Learn more about emails ✕
○	**Calls-to-Action** Create New	Create a call-to-action that you can use on your blog or other site pages to promote your offer.	Learn more about CTAs ✕
○	**Blog Posts** Create New	Feature your campaign as a blog post with a call-to-action for your marketing offer.	Learn more about blog posts ✕

Here is a HubSpot recipe for an ebook campaign, which can help you understand the pieces that are put together for this kind of sequence.

Ebook campaign

This is a typical top-of-the-funnel (TOFU) campaign, designed to help you promote an ebook that you want to use to generate more qualified leads. It includes a sample landing page and form, a thank you message, a promotional email, and a call-to-action.

Landing Page for Ebook

This landing page promotes an ebook and includes a form to capture visitors as leads.

Thank You Page for Ebook

This page thanks your contacts for downloading your ebook.

Follow-up Email for Ebook

This email sends a thank you to anyone who downloads your ebook.

Promo Email for Ebook

This email spreads the word about your ebook.

Call-to-Action to Download Ebook

This call-to-action encourages your website visitors to download your ebook.

Blog Post

This blog post uses a call-to-action to attract more people to your landing page.

Add this recipe

As you start looking at the tools, you start to see some patterns. You might also start to look at websites differently that you visit, recognizing that when you Google something, you might end up on a *landing page (see graphic above)*, and then in return for your contact information, you get an *ebook* download. Then you might get a follow-up email, and some offers for things that may of further interest.

And this is another common campaign "recipe", especially for a service company, for offering a free consultation, as a "magnet" to draw leads further in.

Consultation campaign

This is a typical middle-of-the-funnel (MOFU) campaign designed to further qualify your existing leads and invite them to request a free consultation

Landing Page for Consultation Offer
This landing page gives your middle-of-the-funnel offer a good home.

Thank You Page for Consultation Offer
This page thanks your contacts for requesting a free consultation

Follow-up Email for Consultation Offer
This email sends a thank you to anyone who requests a free consultation

Promotional Email for Consultation Offer
This email extends your consultation offer to your best leads

★ **Call-to-Action for Consultation Offer**
This call-to-action encourages your website visitors to take advantage of your offer.

Add this recipe

On the "front-end", this is what an inbound marketing funnel looks like

rainmakerinternetmarketing.com/services/

ABOUT US   SERVICES   RESOURCES

LEVERAGING THE INTERNET TO MAXIMIZE YOUR ADVERTISING ROI – CALL

INTERNET MARKETING SERVICES

FREE E-BOOK DOWNLOAD: THE 30 GREATEST LEAD GENERATION TIPS, TRICKS & IDEAS

Free E-Book Download

FOCUSED ON LEAD GENERATION

Your business depends upon an ongoing supply of leads and new customers. In today's economy, traditional forms of advertising, like Yellow Pages, do not work like

If you click on Free E-Book Download, you're taken to a form you can fill out.

Download Now: The 30 Greatest Lead Generation Tips, Tricks & Ideas

Tested Tactics for Better Lead Generation

Generating leads - both high in quantity and quality - is a marketers most important objective. A successful lead generation engine is what keeps the funnel full of sales prospects while you sleep

Surprisingly, only 1 in 10 marketers feel their lead generation campaigns are effective. What gives?

There can be a lot of moving parts in any lead generation campaign and often times it's difficult to know which parts need fine tuning. In this guide, we will expose the top 30 techniques marketers should utilize to increase leads and revenue

These tactics have been tested over the past 7 years and have been used by 3,000+ businesses just like yours to generate more than 9.8 million leads last year

Fill Out the Form Below to Grab Your Free Copy!

First name * | Last name
Todd | Kelsey

Email address *
tkelsey@ben.edu

Company Name

Job Title
Professor

Website URL

Describe Yourself *
I own a small business and like ▼

[Download Now!]

Then you receive a download link, but you are still invited to have a free consultation if you'd like one.

Thanks for Downloading!

Here's Your Download Link

You may download your free e-book instantly by clicking this link: http://rainma com/resources/2015/Rainmaker_30-Lead-Generation-Tips-Ebook-Final pdf

Thanks again for your interest, and feel free to bookmark and reference back to this e-book at any time! It's yours forever!

Whether you're looking to expand your presence on the web, or get started altogether, we have lots of resources available. Don't hesitate to reach out to us if you have any questions or would like us to help you take your business to the next level online!

If you would like to request a free consultation, simply fill out the form on the right and we'll get right back to you!

Fill Out the Form Below to Request a Free Consultation

First Name
Todd

Last Name
Kelsey

Company Name

Website URL

Email *
tkelsey@ben.edu

This is all powered by HubSpot, and then it adds contacts into the system for further follow up, showing what actions the new contacts took – such as downloading the ebook. Great! That must mean I'm potentially interested.

HubSpot Pricing/Features

As mentioned before, there are different "tiers" of HubSpot. You can get into HubSpot for as little as $200/month, but you will be limited to only 100 contacts and several automation features will be missing.

What I'd recommend is visiting this page, and looking at the difference between the Basic plan (currently $200/month annually), and the Professional plan ($800/month annually).

http://www.hubspot.com/pricing-comparison

Note: Sales and Marketing

One thing to note – we're just scratching the surface here, and this book is generally oriented towards a beginning audience, on the marketing side of things. But it's helpful to know that for a business with salespeople, marketing automation systems such as Infusionsoft and HubSpot and others can be used by both sales and marketing staff.

For example, in a B2B situation, an ad campaign, and email campaign may be set in motion to generate leads, and the automation systems can notify salespeople to follow up on the leads. Within the CRM portion of the system, salespeople can "Drill down" to a contact record, and see how far along they are in the funnel, what actions they've taken, what "segment" they're in, and so on.

Industry Perspective: Tools of the Trade

	Bill Crawford, *Founder and President of* *Rainmaker Internet Marketing*

Todd: So at what point should a small or medium-sized business consider a marketing automation tool?

Bill: Some businesses start right out of the gate with MA. But the answer is "whenever it makes sense."

It makes sense typically when the business owner is ready to grow the business and take it to the next level. We have seen it more successful when employees are open to embrace the change. Furthermore, it works even better when a key employee is willing to embrace and take ownership of the new technology. Having worked with owners in the past, owners get busy and distracted too frequently for them to be the CRM owner, so to speak. They need to make room in their schedule to embrace the new technology. As we all know, it is common to underestimate the time it takes to learn something new.

When you start working with local service providers, what are the typical tools they use for keeping track of their contact information?

Many still have a written down system. Some use Excel and Outlook. Some have a half baked software system someone internally tried to make. Some have Zoho, Constant Contact, etc.

If you want to work with marketing automation, do you have to give up your email tool or your CRM? How do you know whether to integrate to a new tool or replace?

Great questions. I've seen people move to an integrated suite (email, ecommerce, marketing automation, CRM, etc.) because they look at the variety of tools they are using, add up the cost, and realize it is less expensive as well as more efficient to work with just one software. The best answer really is - it depends. It depends what they have and what they are going to plug into. But increasingly various tools are offering integrations so that if it makes sense, you're more likely to be able to continue using an existing tool if you like it.

From what you've seen, based on pricing and capability, at what point is it good for a company to consider a tool like Infusionsoft, vs a tool like HubSpot?

The owner should consider how much time and money they are wasting by not being organized. How much time do they spend looking for things. Also, consider how many prospects are not being followed up on. And consider much would sales and profit increase if more prospects were turned into sales. Many of the customer success stories for marketing automation include an increase in leads, overall revenue, and in some cases, a reduced number of hours that the business owner ends up having to work, as things are automated over time. The systems don't automatically or magically do the work for you – it takes work, and commitment, but the results can be significant and the increase in revenue can pay for the system.

Have you seen businesses that have justified the cost of investment in Infusionsoft? How about HubSpot?

Absolutely – you can see examples of this in some of the case studies later in the book.

What's your perspective about the value of Inbound Marketing (drawing people in), vs Outbound marketing (ex: Adwords)? How do you strike a balance between the two?

To hit your maximum revenue potential, you typically need both. The exact balance depends on the business model and industry.

Btw, inbound marketing often gets compared to more traditional forms: telemarketing, cold calling, canvassing. It also gets contrasted to media buys; TV, radio, newspaper. The philosophy of inbound recognizes that people are FLOODED with marketing messages, therefore they tune it all out. For that reason, traditional marketing becomes very ineffective. Inbound marketing says - people will contact you when they are good and ready and they will typically find you online.

Conclusion/Discussion

Congratulations on making it through the third chapter, and getting to know two more tools of the trade!

You've gotten some exposure to leading marketing platforms, and you've seen some of the techniques you can use to make custom automation sequences. In the next section, we'll dive into some "hands on" work so you can get a concrete sense of what marketing automation is all about.

If you're ready to take things to the next level, you're also welcome to schedule a free consultation, to see how Rainmaker Internet Marketing can help your business make use of marketing automation. Please visit rainma.com/automation

Learning More

Here's some links to get you started.

Infusionsoft

www.infusionsoft.com

http://www.infusionsoft.com/success-stories
> A good set of case studies to show how marketing automation impacted peoples' businesses

https://www.youtube.com/watch?v=yN1lpp43Pz4
> A nice video about Iron Tribe Fitness, who leveraged Infusionsoft to the max.

HubSpot

www.hubspot.com

http://www.hubspot.com/customers
> case studies of how marketing automation material is used.

What is HubSpot?
https://www.youtube.com/watch?v=X_bqIr7pGzQ
2 min

For More Information

For a complete list of links and resources, visit rainma.com/book

Chapter 4: Hands On – Make a Free Web Site/Blog

Introduction

In this chapter, we'll be taking a look at the foundation of marketing automation – which is having a Web site. This chapter is particularly for readers who'd like to know more about websites, and the various options for creating them. I think that for any business owner, it's also a good idea to know some of the basics of working with content on the Web.

Business owners will probably want to take a look at the section at the end of this chapter for some Industry Perspective on Wordpress – there's a free version of it, but it also happens to be the leading platform at the moment for paid websites.

To a certain extent, the principle applies – you get what you pay for. But on the other hand, sometimes you might wish to make a Web site as an extra project, or for a friend, or even just as a prototype, where the paid platforms aren't necessary.

In this chapter, I'm using Google Sites as an example. There are other tools out there (see the "other systems" section below), but Google Sites happens to be very easy to use, so I use it in all the classes I teach.

When you're reading this book, if you're ready to take things to the next level, you're also welcome to schedule a free consultation, to see how Rainmaker Internet Marketing can help your business make use of marketing automation. Please visit rainma.com/automation

Create a Google Account/Gmail address

Google has a lot of free tools that make it easier to work with content, and when you have a Google Account, it just makes it easier to sign in to all the tools. So when you follow this chapter, technically you could use a different email address to create a Google account, but I recommend just creating a Gmail address; it just makes everything easier. (Note: you can always forward Gmail to your other email, or use your new Gmail address to "check" your old email.)

So as a first step, I recommend creating a free Google Account by going to http://mail.google.com and clicking "Create Account".

Create a Free Website with Google Sites

My general recommendation as you learn about marketing automation is to try some or all of the pieces of it out yourself, including even making your own website. Furthermore, Google Sites and other free tools can be excellent tools for "prototyping" a site. Let's say you get something started, and you end up using a freelancer or agency at some point – it is still helpful to assemble content as you can, such as pictures, writing some text, etc., even if you end up going "professional" later, so that you can have something to demonstrate some of what you're looking for.

Another thing to keep in mind about free marketing tools is that they can be used to create microsites – that is, a small brochure type site, with a focused marketing message, purely to support a specific campaign. That can be helpful to have as an alternative tool, to dedicated landing page tools, which serve a similar purpose. (See www.leadpages.net)

Blogs vs Websites

A blog technically is a website, and blogging platforms such as Wordpress (www.wordpress.com – free and paid versions), have grown to the point where they can serve as fully-functional websites, depending on how you organize them.

But it can be simpler at first to think of a blog as a place you post "ongoing" content, such as a library of articles, and your "main site" is the reference material that may not change as often, whether it's for a business or organization.

I recommend you try making a Google site, and keep it as part of your arsenal. You might even want to have a Google Site be "your" main site, such as your freelance business, etc. – with basic information.

> NOTE ABOUT WEBSITE NAMES: with Blogger, and Google Sites, even though you choose a custom "long" address provided by Google, you can also use your own website name. Website hosting companies will sell you website names, or web "hosting" space, where a traditional site can be built using HTML, etc. – another advantage of Google Sites or Blogger is that they're entirely free, but you can still point your website name to them. A website name like www.toddkelsey.com may cost only $10 a year, kind of like a copyright, whereas a website hosting account, to do a manually-created website, might start at $10/month. As for me, what I noticed over time is that for some simple sites, I preferred Google Sites, because it allowed me to easily post content, there was no monthly cost, and it was basically more sustainable.
>
> And having your own website name comes across slightly more professionally – so you might want to file that away. You can look for names on websites like www.godaddy.com, and start an account (a website name such as www.toddkelsey.com is also known as a "domain" name). And then you can "point" your website name to your blogger blog or google site. If you end up wanting to try that, I'd suggest looking into the help sections on blogger and google sites about "web addresses".

Creating a Site

So, to get started, go to: http://sites.google.com

Log in if you need to, or click the create account button.

Like Blogger, Google Sites packs a lot of power. The other advantage of keeping in mind sites like Blogger and Google Sites, is if you're not a developer, you don't need to have technical skills in order to make websites using these tools. So it might be a good alternative for a client where you can provide the service of focusing on the content for the site or marketing, and can whip up a site, without necessarily having to hire a web developer. There are limits, of course, but it can also be a starting point. For example, use Google Sites to gather content to begin with, organize, and "prototype" – and then when you have a better idea of where things are going, hire a designer/web developer, or get costs and let your client choose.

Next, click the Create button.

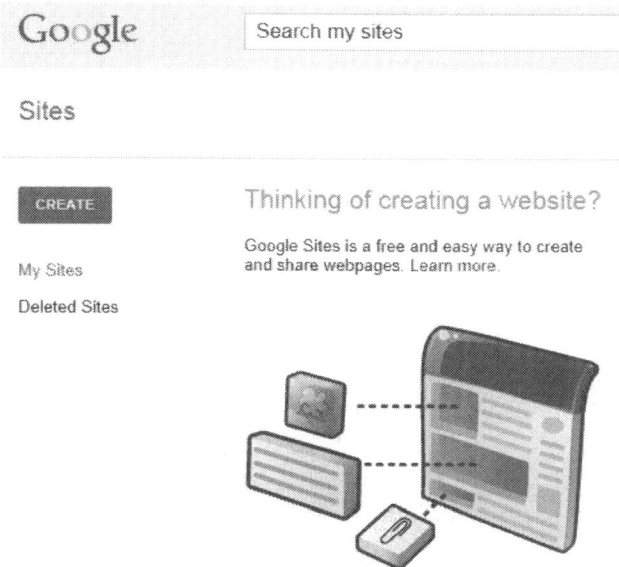

(If you're taking it for granted how easy it is, try going to Godaddy.com, looking at how much effort is required to start a hosting account, get a website started, either with a content management system like Drupal, a "website builder", or even using a manual tool like Dreamweaver. I guarantee after trying that, you'll appreciate how much time you're saving by just being able to click "create". Thanks, Google.)

There are some pre-built templates you can choose from – in Google Sites it is a little more tricky to go back and change things later, so until you explore how you can customize things, I'd recommend choosing the Blank template at first.

So you select the template, and then you have to choose an address, just like you do in Blogger.

Select a template to use:

Blank template Classroom site 🔍 Soccer team 🔍 Spring Floral Wedding Instructional 🔍

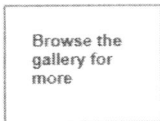

Browse the gallery for more

Name your site:

You can click in the Name your site field, and type in a name, which is like a title, and can be changed easily later. Then you'll have to experiment and try different "site location" names. You can also click on Select a theme, or "more options", but to begin with I'd suggest keeping it simple. (In Google Sites, the "themes" are what you can come back and easily change later, which provide some basic customization in look and feel).

Name your site:

socialmicrosite

Site location - URLs can only use the following characters: A-Z,a-z,0-9
https://sites.google.com/site/   socialmicrosite

▸ Select a theme
▸ More options

Type the code shown:

bitsu &

CREATE

You'll also have to type in the code (ex: "bitsu" above), before you can click the Create button.

As you're typing in site location names, Google may tell you that the one you want isn't available, and you might have to experiment:

Site location - URLs can only use the following characters: A-Z,a-z,0-9

https://sites.google.com/site/ `mysite` ✕

The location you have chosen is not available. Learn more...

And then – voila! You have a new website.

To learn more about Google Sites, go to either of these links, which point to the same place:
https://support.google.com/sites/?hl=en#topic=1689606

http://tinyurl.com/googsite-help
My basic recommendation is to try making a site, including one for yourself, for your portfolio, etc. – or try making one for a potential client, such as an imaginary local business – or a promotional campaign of some kind.

Other Low-Cost/Free Systems

A couple more options that are popular, and have free/paid options for making website:
http://wix.com

http://weebly.com

http://www.strikingly.com – I particularly like this one, and created several sites recently with it – I like the professional look and feel, the fact it was mobile responsive, etc. Ex. site: http://npoex.com

http://www.squarespace.com – a friend recommended taking a look at Squarespace – he liked the templates and various features that come with the platform. See http://www.markneal.org as an example site.

Create a Blog

There are a variety of platforms for blogging, but blogger.com is one of the easiest to use, if not the easiest.

The reason to try creating a blog, is related to the "marketing automation ecosystem" that we talked about earlier in the book, as well as the concept of "inbound marketing". The bottom line is, that having a blog on your site in some way is one of the best ways of attracting traffic to your site "organically", by posting relevant information that might be helpful to your target audience. Blogging also gives you material to post to social media, etc.

If you're interested in developing a social media marketing and/or inbound marketing strategy, my general suggestion is to create a blog, and set the goal of posting to it at least once a month (or more often). Choose a topic or tool you're learning about, or a technique you're interested in, do some research, gather some links, and get in the habit of developing some ongoing posts.

Just as with a "main website", a simple free blog might be a way to get some content developed, which you could then use in a website redesign. If you are playing with free tools such as Google Sites, technically you could just add pages/articles to Google Sites, for example – but a blog can be even simpler to manage – you can just go on and add posts.

Making the Blog

So to get started, visit http://www.blogger.com, and either sign in with your Google account, or click the "create an account" link at the bottom.

Google

One account. All of Google.

Sign in to continue to Blogger

Email

Password

Sign in

☑ Stay signed in   Need help?

Create an account

Then on the blogger site, click the New Blog button.

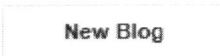

New Blog

For practice, I wouldn't be too concerned with the title – you can change it later easily, and you can also create/delete blogs easily.

Blogs List › Create a new blog

Title   Social Media Perspective

Address   .blogspot.com

                              You can add a custom domain later.

The title is simply what appears visually at the top of the blog. The "Address" is the opportunity Google gives you to have a custom address. Because it's a free tool, you might have to experiment a bit until you find one that's available. Type in ideas in the Address field, and see what happens:

socialbuzz| .blogspot.com   !

Sorry, this blog address is not available.

What you're doing is coming up with the custom portion of the address that you're blog will be at.

socialbuzznews| .blogspot.com   ✓

This blog address is available.

So it turns out for our example, the address socialbuzznews.blogspot.com is available.

So the link for the blog would be http://socialbuzznews.blogspot.com

Then after you have chosen a title and address, you can choose a template, for the look and feel of the blog, which you can also change later:

Blogs List › Create a new blog

Title	Social Media Perspective
Address	socialbuzznews| .blogspot.com ✓

This blog address is available.

Template

Simple   Dynamic Views   Picture Window

Awesome Inc.   Watermark   Ethereal

You can browse many more templates and customize your blog later.

Create blog!   Cancel

After you've selected one (I recommend starting with "Simple"), click the **Create blog!** button.

With these simple steps, you've created a blog and you can start blogging!

You're mission if you should choose to accept it is to make a sample post, and then share the link on Facebook, or via email with someone.

New Blog   Social Media Perspective   View blog

Your Blog has been created! Start posting | Dismiss

P.S. One way to "cheat" if you forget the link for your blog, is to click on the View blog button (See screenshot above), which will open up the blog in your browser. Then you can copy the link from the address field and paste it into Facebook, or an email, etc.

To learn more about Blogger, access the settings menu (the little gear icon) when you're signed into Blogger, and select "Blogger Help":

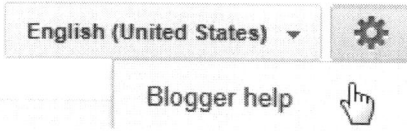

There's a variety of helpful articles:

And you can always go directly with this link:

https://support.google.com/blogger

Industry Perspective: Web Site Platforms

Brian Glassman
Account Manager, Lead Designer
Rainmaker Internet Marketing

Todd: For digital marketing, how important is a website for your business? What are the main considerations to look for?

Brian: The first think to look for is whether or not your website does a good job of passing "The Blink Test." The Blink Test is a powerful term used in the marketing world to describe how long businesses have to hook users into their site and keep them from hitting that dreaded "Close" button. That's right, just a few seconds—or "blink." But passing the Blink Test is no simple task—users are very impatient when it comes to websites and have developed very high standards in recent years.

To ensure your website does a good job of hooking your audience in, make sure it loads fast (2-3 seconds), has a visually pleasing design, clearly explains what you do/offer, and is easy to navigate.

Learn more:
http://blog.hubspot.com/blog/tabid/6307/bid/34061/How-to-Make-Sure-Your-Website-Passes-the-Dreaded-Blink-Test.aspx

And if you're not sure how long people spend on your page before leaving, that's where Google Analytics comes in. Make sure it is installed on your site so you can look at "time on site" and other factors. Integrating Google Analytics is a crucial part of any website design or redesign, even though it's in the background. See www.google.com/analytics

If you were starting from scratch, or considering doing a re-design, what are the main considerations for choosing a web platform, from a marketing automation perspective?

Flexibility and user experience are important here. Plugging marketing automation into a website typically involves embedding special blocks of code, creating new pages, and other important website configurations. If you're not a web developer these tasks can prove to be difficult—if not impossible.

This is where a CMS like Wordpress shines. (CMS = Content Management Systems). Traditionally, web sites have been built from scratch using thousands and thousands of lines of hand-written code. A CMS takes all that complicated background code, and transforms the process of building a website into an easy-to-use interface, so you can build your website without having to be a super-nerd (well, it's still a little nerdy but much easier)!

We recommend using WordPress.

What are the most important things to keep in mind for other aspects of digital marketing, in terms of the capability a web platform should have?

Well, one of the biggest benefits of Content Management Systems is they take out a lot of the challenge of website building by hiding the complicated background code behind a nice and easy-to-use user interface.

However, that ease of use can also be detrimental to your digital marketing and automation goals. For example, some content management systems are very restrictive in what they allow you to modify, making it impossible to do certain tasks without either modifying the background code or reaching out to the CMS service provider.

So you need to strike a balance between ease of use, and flexibility.

Why is Wordpress your platform of choice? Do you have any favorite templates?

WordPress, in my opinion, strikes the right balance between user-friendly and developer-friendly.

For example, if I wanted to I could build a complete website using a beautiful pre-designed theme/template, use only the built-in WordPress editor, install a few plug-ins, and be all set!

But if I wanted to dive in and extend functionality or get a little fancy, I also have access to the back-end code, and a variety of developer plug-ins that allow me to perform advanced website configurations.

What is a WordPress "Plug-in"? What are you favorite plug-ins, for functionality, SEO, security?

Plug-ins are essentially extra applications that "plug" into on your existing WordPress installation. One of the benefits of using WordPress is taking advantage of the huge developer community, which has collectively published over 38,000 plug-ins!

For security, I recommend the BruteProtect and Limit Login Attempts plug-ins. These plug-ins prevent hackers and spam robots from forcing their way in and making modifications to your website. You may also want to install a security scan plugin called Sucuri Scanner. This plug-in will scan your existing Wordpress installation for malware, vulnerabilities, and even tell you if your site has been blacklisted by search engines.

My favorite SEO plug-in is Wordpress SEO by Yoast for a variety of reasons. First and foremost, it's easy to use. You can easily add title tags, meta descriptions, alter the title tag format, configure index (search engine readability) settings, and even get a search snippet character counter/preview. It's also really powerful, and unlocks lots of handy features for a power user such as myself.

What about tools like Weebly, Wix, and Google Sites? Can you just do my site on those tools?

You absolutely can. Just note that these solutions have some limitations, and may be "overly" user-friendly. They're easy to use, but have fewer customization options. If you're looking for deeper customization and more control of your site, these options may not be for you.

If you already have a website name at (mywebsite.com, etc.), can you "re-point" it if you do a redesign?

You're going to need 2 things in order to publish a website. First, you'll need a domain. Your domain name is the "address" of your website online. For example, google.com is Google's domain name. To purchase a new domain name, I recommend GoDaddy.com.

Second, you'll need hosting. A website is essentially a collection folders and files stored on a server (large, internet-connected hard drive); so in order to publish your website, you'll need to purchase service space in the form of a Hosting package. Hosting packages can be purchased through GoDaddy, BlueHost, Host Gator, and a variety of other companies. When you get a hosting package, you can get various kinds of "servers", which is the operating system your website runs on. For maximum flexibility and compatibility, I recommend using a Linux Server (as opposed to a Windows server).

While most businesses find it easier to manage everything in one place, such as registering a name at godaddy and also having the website itself hosted at GoDaddy -- you do not need to have your domains and hosting packages living in the same place. If you develop a brand new website on a new server, all you need to do is "re-point" the website name at the new location.

How does keeping up with changes on Google relate - for example, what's the big deal about having a mobile-friendly website and how do you do it on Wordpress?

Search engines like Google and Bing are constantly evolving. The field of digital marketing is a moving target, so if you don't have your eye on the ball, you'll find your business (and your website) falling behind.

Google's big Mobile-Friendly algorithm update, which deployed on April 21st, 2015, essentially meant that if your website wasn't "mobile-friendly," you'd be cast aside in the mobile search engine rankings in favor of your more mobile-friendly competitors. You can imagine the panic this caused in the larger marketing world, as clients began clamoring for redesigned, responsive (automatically adjusts to be mobile-friendly) websites.

In regards to Wordpress, the iPhone catchphrase applies: "There's an App for that". If there's a need for some tool on a Wordpress website, you guessed it: "there's a plug-in for that." With a simple search, you can install one of a variety of mobile-friendly Wordpress plug-ins—some free, some paid—to ensure your site is mobile-friendly. There are also thousands of responsive Wordpress themes you can install on your site that will give your site a great new look, with the added benefit of being responsive and mobile-friendly. (Responsive means automatically resizing for different size screens and formats.)

Conclusion/Discussion

Congratulations on making it through the fourth chapter, and getting some hands-on experience!

You've gotten some exposure to creating a free website, and learned about the value of using free tools to assemble content, even if you end up hiring someone to design your Website. In the next chapter, we'll dive into MailChimp, and a take a look at how to create an email list – a crucial part of any marketing automation strategy, no matter what tools you use.

If you're ready to take things to the next level, you're also welcome to schedule a free consultation, to see how Rainmaker Internet Marketing can help your business make use of marketing automation. Please visit rainma.com/automation

Learning More

Here's some links to get you started.

Google Sites

To learn more about Google Sites, go to either of these links, which point to the same place:
https://support.google.com/sites/?hl=en#topic=1689606

http://tinyurl.com/googsite-help

Other Systems

http://wix.com

http://weebly.com

http://www.strikingly.com – I particularly like this one, and created several sites recently with it – I like the professional look and feel, the fact it was mobile responsive, etc. Ex. site: http://npoex.com

http://www.squarespace.com – a friend recommended taking a look at Squarespace – he liked the templates and various features that come with the platform. See http://www.markneal.org as an example site.

For More Information

For a complete list of links and resources, visit rainma.com/book

Chapter 5: Hands On – Starting an Email List

Introduction

In this chapter, we'll be taking a look at how to set up an email list in MailChimp, so you can get a concrete sense of the foundation of marketing automation – contact information.

When you're reading this book, if you're ready to take things to the next level, you're also welcome to schedule a free consultation, to see how Rainmaker Internet Marketing can help your business make use of marketing automation. Please visit rainma.com/automation

Starting an Account

To start an account, visit www.mailchimp.com and click on the Sign Up button:

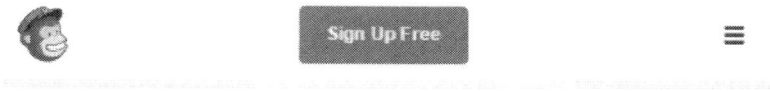

Then fill out your email, come up with a username, and a password, and click Create My Account:

Get started with a Free Account

Sign up in 30 seconds. No credit card required.
Already have a MailChimp account? Log in here.

Email

What's your email address?

Username

Password

[Show]

- One lowercase character
- One uppercase character
- One number
- One special character
- Eight characters minimum

[Create My Account]

Then you'll need to check your email and activate the account.

Thanks For Signing Up!
Please check your email and click **Activate Account** in the message we just sent to todd.e.kelsey@gmail.com.

Once your account is activated, we'll send you an email with some information to help you get started with MailChimp.

Activation/Configuration

When you activate, there's some basic information you need to put in that has an impact on your email list. Start by entering your first and last name.

Let's Get Started

About You

First name

Last name

Email address

todd.e.kelsey@gmail.com

Your email address will remain private. Our privacy policy

Then scroll down and fill out the Organization Info – if you try to skip it like I did, they'll bring you back.

Organization Information

These questions will help us tailor MailChimp to you in the future.

About how many people are in your organization?

Select

Please enter a value

About how old is your organization?

Select

Please enter a value

Do you have a list of emails to import into MailChimp?

Select

Please enter a value

Are you setting this up for a client?

Select

Please enter a value

This next section is important – things can be changed later, but this is what will automatically appear on the signup form, and the website you put here will be the one that the signup form will re-direct to:

Company / organization

RGB Press

Website URL

http://www.rgbpress.net

No website?

Address 1

P.O. Box 1302

Address 2

City

Wheaton

State / Province / Region

Il

Zip / Postal code

60187

Country

USA

Next, select a Time zone:

Time zone

When you schedule campaigns, we'll use this time zone as a reference.

Time zone

(GMT -5:00) Central Time

I ignored the Profile Photo option, but I do recommend subscribing to the Mailchimp Getting Started emails.

Profile Photo

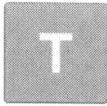

Upload your photo …
Photo should be at least 300px × 300px

Upload Photo   **Take A Photo!**

☐ **Subscribe to MailChimp Getting Started Emails, a series of emails to help you transform from beginner to pro.**

Save And Get Started

Then click the Save and Get Started button.

After you enter that basic information, you'll be returned to a screen, probably the Dashboard.

Campaigns   Templates   Lists   Reports   Automation   Todd RGB Press   Help

Dashboard

Create Campaign

Get started

Create and send a campaign
Campaigns are emails sent to subscribers in a list. Try your hand at email design by creating and sending a test campaign. learn more

Create A Campaign

Create a list
Lists are where you store your contacts (we call them subscribers). Create one master list, then use segments and groups to email select people. learn more

Create A List

Start building your audience
Signup forms let people subscribe to your list. When you create a list we'll automatically build a signup form to customize for your website, Facebook, iPad and more. learn more

Create A List

Invite your colleagues
Every MailChimp account can have multiple users, collaborating together to build campaigns, manage lists and analyze reports. Invite other people to join your account. learn more

Invite Users

Guide to getting started with MailChimp

Read our guide online, or download the ePub or PDF for reading on your tablet.

In particular, you may want to click on the "Read our guide" link at the below, to get their PDF, or learn from their site directly. The link is also at the end of the chapter and here: http://mailchimp.com/resources/guides/getting-started-with-mailchimp/

Starting a List

To start a list, go www.mailchimp.com, and log in:

In theory, you'll see a dashboard, and if not, you can click on "Lists" at the top:

Next, click the Create a List button:

Create a list

Lists are where you store your contacts (we call them subscribers). Create one master list, then use segments and groups to email select people. learn more

Create A List

On the list screen, click the Create List button:

Create List

Here's where you can fill in the details. You can make more than one list, so I'd suggest making a sample list.

List details

List name

RGB Press

Default "from" email

todd.e.kelsey@gmail.com

Default "from" name

Todd Kelsey

You may want to consider making a separate email address like info@yourcompany.com, and making sure that the email address forwards to your main account. You might also want to make a new Gmail address like yourcompanyinfo@gmail.com – and then go in and have it forward to your main email account. And either way, you could put that email address here (or come back and change it later).

Then you'll want to scroll down and add in a reminder statement (it's part of etiquette, and also compliance with the CAN-SPAM Act).

Remind people how they got on your list

> You are receiving this email because you opted in to join our email list.

Contact information for this list · Why is this necessary?

> **RGB Press**
> P.O. Box 1302
> Wheaton, Il 60187

Edit

Next, you can click the checkboxes for notifications you might want – I'd suggest clicking all of them until you get tired of receiving the notifications.

Notifications Sent to todd.e.kelsey@gmail.com · Edit

☐ **Daily summary**
Summary of subscribe/unsubscribe activity

☐ **One-by-one**
Subscribe notifications as they happen

☐ **One-by-one**
Unsubscribe notifications as they happen

Save   Cancel

Get Back to Where You Once Belong

Now that you've set up a list, if you ever want to get back to it, you can log into Mailchimp and click on the Lists option.

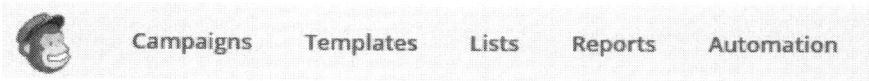

Campaigns   Templates   Lists   Reports   Automation

See your Email List in Action

Now it's time to test your email list, and see things in action. Hats off to Mailchimp for making all these moving pieces relatively easy to set up, with a system that keeps track of things for you, and free! (Free up to a certain point – the # of subscribers – but reasonably priced).

So, log into Mailchimp, go to Lists, and on the Lists page, click the downward arrow next to "Stats":

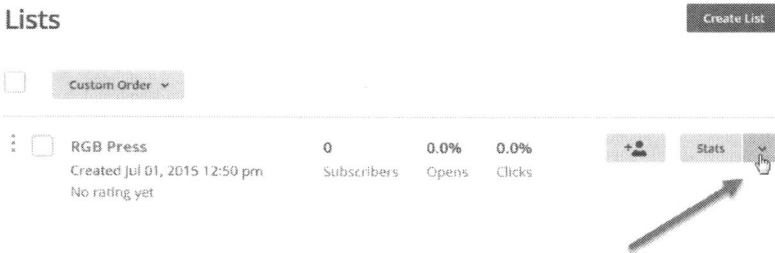

Lists   Create List

Custom Order ˅

RGB Press   0   0.0%   0.0%   +&   Stats
Created Jul 01, 2015 12:50 pm   Subscribers   Opens   Clicks
No rating yet

Next, choose the Signup forms option. We're going to get the link for your form that Mailchimp created, and try it out.

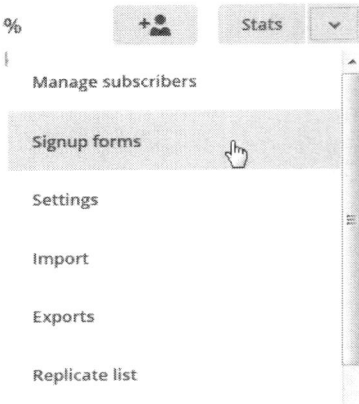

Look in the list of forms, and click the Select button next to "General Forms":

Here, there's some options – there's no right or wrong answer; I'd suggest trying the options of letting subscribers pick their email format. Most people can read HTML email, but some companies filter it so that people need to read plaintext versions. (When you do this, be aware that Mailchimp may create an "automatic" plaintext version when you send out an email, but make a note to check and edit it – easy to forget)

I'd also suggest trying the reCAPTCHA option – it's one more thing people have to do when signing up, but it makes the form more secure, slightly less vulnerable to spam.

Create Forms

Forms and response emails

| Signup form | ▾ |

[ ] Let subscribers pick email format (plain-text or HTML)

(i) Info

[ ] Protect your signup form with reCAPTCHA

(i) Info

Signup form URL

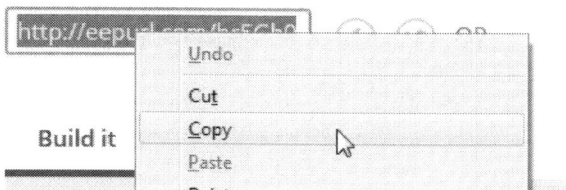

| http://eepurl.com/br5Gb9 | (f) (🐦) QR

Next, you'll want to make a note of the "Signup form URL". This is a link you can email, post on the web, social media, etc., for inviting people to sign up for your email list.

NOTE: As we'll see in the next chapter, you can embed the email list signup form on a web page – but it's still helpful to know you can link directly to it.

I suggest clicking in the Signup form URL field, and then right clicking (Windows) or CTRL+click (Mac) and copy the address, and make a note of it somewhere.

Signup form URL

http://eepu...	Undo
	Cut
	Copy
Build it	Paste

In this editor screen, if you like, you can "click to add a message", such as "Please join our email list! We'll only email occasionally, and you can unsubscribe anytime."

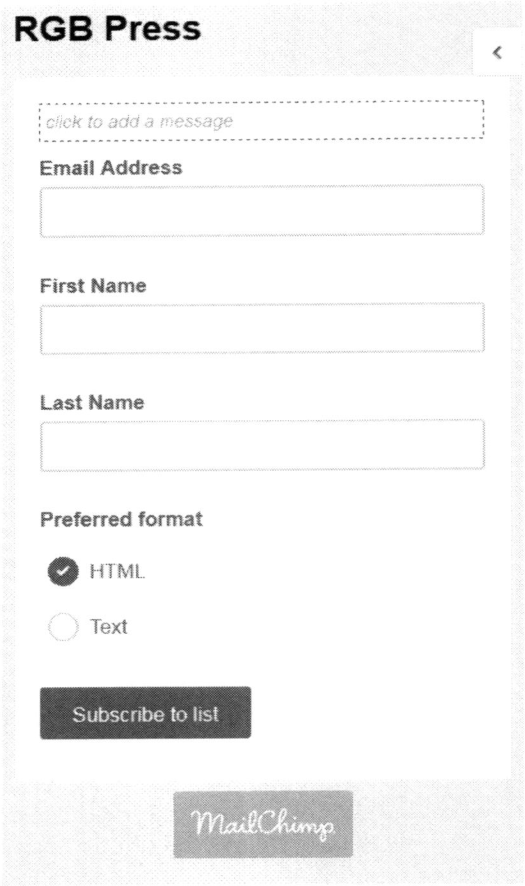

RGB Press

‹

click to add a message

Email Address

First Name

Last Name

Preferred format

✓ HTML

○ Text

Subscribe to list

MailChimp

Now, go to the link for your email list, to test it out.

Or, try the one I made: http://eepurl.com/br5Gb9

Depending on the settings you chose, it will look pretty simple (yes, you can customize if you like). And the link in the browser will be something like:
http://rgbpress.us11.list-manage.com/subscribe?u=6011bfe0c68707a8fa022c064&id=b3d1d44017

So I'd suggest going ahead and signing up for your own list. It will go through the confirmation screen, and it will display the contact information you placed when you signed up. If you put your personal contact information, I'd suggest getting a P.O. Box or otherwise using the business address. If you can't figure out where to change the information in MailChimp, they have a helpful support crew.

Then it's also worth noting that when you click on the return to our website button, it will take you to whatever website you indicated when you started the account. So you'll want to proactively think about what link to put in there, and it can be different for each list, etc. In this case it goes back to:

http://www.rgbpress.net

Looking Ahead

Now that you've made a simple email list, I encourage you to try making a few mailings, sharing the link around with friends and family, even if it's just a test, to see how things work. Then, I invite you to look further into Mailchimp's capabilities, especially if you've never had an email list before. Experimenting with some of Mailchimp's built-in features can help you get comfortable with some of the concepts that apply to more sophisticated marketing automation tools, such as Infusionsoft or HubSpot.

Also, I invite you particularly to take a look at MailChimp's "Marketing Automation Workflows" video, to get a taste of the kinds of things Mailchimp can do.

The link is available here, as well as at the end of the chapter:
https://www.youtube.com/watch?v=NuftV4sp99M

Industry Perspective: Email and CRM Systems

Bill Crawford,
Founder and President of
Rainmaker Internet Marketing

Todd: What are the most typical email systems your clients use for email and CRM?

Bill: Outlook is the most common email system. As small businesses embrace more technology, a next step is often Mailchimp or Constant Contact. Some use industry specific CRM systems while others use some listed in the link below:

http://www.capterra.com/customer-relationship-management-software/#infographic

At the present time, SalesForce and Oracle are NOT typical small business local service provider CRMs, because of their complexity and cost – but that could change in the future.

Another common "all-in-one" system is Zoho. www.zoho.com

I think it's also helpful to review things that didn't work. Here's an interesting article definitely worth looking at – on *terrible* CRM systems:
http://www.forbes.com/sites/quickerbettertech/2013/07/01/11-terrible-crm-systems-for-your-company

Todd: Do local service providers often need both an email system, "and" a CRM system? What's the value proposition?

Bill: As the cost of technology has dropped and becomes more user friendly, local service providers have found email and CRM systems have provided a way to get more organized and have better follow up. Modern systems also can provide a way to follow up specifically based on the habits of their customer, so that the message and follow up is increasingly personalized, that is, going from "one-sized fits all" to a more custom approach. That can result in greater response. This is often referred to as market segmentation – in HubSpot's case they talk about customer personas – when you take the time to tailor different messages for different parts of your customer base, you can get a better customer response.

The answer on email system vs CRM systems is "it depends" – partly on the system. Some email systems have increased capabilities to send messages out to different parts of the list – "segmentation". Some email systems are starting to offer marketing automation as well. So you could just develop an email list, and send out "one-sized fits all" messages, and if your email system supports it, you can experiment with making custom messages, but generally, systems that grew out of email management are not as good at dedicated systems for a particular task.

The CRM system is generally the basis for customer follow up – often "live" follow up, such as a sales force having a central way to keep track of customers, potential customers.

Then, when you're talking about marketing automation, either features within an email or CRM system, or a dedicated marketing automation system, or an "all in one" solution like Infusionsoft, then generally the value that the system provides is to make your life easier when you're ready to take your business to the next level. So you might try to manage everything yourself, and there are cases where local services providers have struggled to manage all the moving pieces and try to grow at the same time, or even be competitive; but then with an investment in a marketing automation system, and with an investment of time, they've found that automating a lot of the stuff they tried to do allowed them to concentrate on growing the business.

Todd: Why is it important to have advanced email management capability?

Bill: This allows for automation. Automation, when set up correctly provides everything mentioned above; better follow up, specific follow up based on previous habits, and can save the owner time and help them get more organized. A big feature is - this supports the age old business truth that it generally is much less expensive to retain or "up sell" an existing customer than it is to obtain a new one.

Todd: How often should you send emails to current customers? What kinds of things can a local service provider send? What's the most effective?

Bill: What is best to understand is email addresses are still the most fought after piece of real estate in America. Companies want email addresses because they know this is an extremely inexpensive form of advertising and when they are reading your email, you have more of their attention than at any other time. If they are reading something on the Internet, there are always other things trying to get their attention. Not so, with an email.

Also, your content ideally needs to be 80% high quality helpful content / 20% sales. If you are too salesy, people tune you out.

With automation, a common email sequence in the first month is a welcome campaign which includes things like; how to reach us if you ever need help, meet the staff, tips of the service or product they purchased, an NPS survey after 30 days which spills into a referral request or customer review request. (NPS = Net Promoter Score; see www.netpromoter.com)

Some companies have success in sending out a once a month/quarter Big Bargain sales; and reminders are always useful; depending on the purchase.

Todd: How does "lead generation" relate to having an email system in place? Do you need a form on your website to get peoples' emails?

Bill: Having a form on your website is a very useful way to obtain email addresses. Typically there is an exchange that occurs; I'll give you this amazing something (e-book, cheat sheet, video, kit, white paper, etc.) but you will need to provide me with your email address. This strategy is a good way to begin a relationship with prospects. It is low risk in that no money is being exchanged and the prospect gets further introduced to your service. All they have to do is give up their email address and nowadays, most folks have a spare email address just for this reason.

Todd: What's the best way to get people to give you their contact information? Does having a marketing automation tool make a difference?

Bill: Offer something compelling to your prospect.

Automation sure does make it easier. Automation allows for instant delivery and specific follow up. Automation will notify you when the prospect is ready to be contacted.

Todd: Would you recommend getting a CRM system first, and then a marketing automation tool?

Bill: Since the price of marketing automation is so low, I would recommend starting with this. No one uses all the features of marketing automation but you can use this software as a CRM and learn it as you go.

Todd: Can CRM systems do everything? Email, empower the sales force, and marketing automation too?

Bill: It's my understanding that most CRM's do *not* do marketing automation. In fact, the phrase "marketing automation" is defined *very* loosely. Consumer beware! For example, I've seen companies fire off a single email and say they have marketing automation. And I have seen other companies do automated things that are mind blowing - with the same phrase 'marketing automation'. So it's probably good to learn what the most sophisticated systems can do, look at case studies of how people have used them, businesses like yours, and what they've achieved. And then measure systems against those examples and features.

Conclusion/Discussion

Congratulations on making it through the fifth chapter, and making an email list!

You've gotten some exposure to capturing and managing email lists, and you've seen first-hand how tools can manage a lot of the process for you, such as hosting a form, making sure you're complying with SPAM legislation, etc.

In the next chapter, we'll revisit the blog and website you created, and show how you can take an email list, and connect it your website. This will give you a sense of how you can connect various parts of the "marketing automation ecosystem". There's a variety of ways to accomplish acquiring and managing contact information, and we'll keep it simple.

If you're ready to take things to the next level, you're also welcome to schedule a free consultation, to see how Rainmaker Internet Marketing can help your business make use of marketing automation. Please visit rainma.com/automation

Learning More

Here's some links to get you started.

MailChimp Getting Started
http://mailchimp.com/resources/guides/getting-started-with-mailchimp/

MailChimp Automation Guide
http://mailchimp.com/resources/guides/working-with-automation

For More Information

For a complete list of links and resources, visit rainma.com/book

Chapter 6: Hands On - Collecting Contact Info on Your Blog or Site

Introduction

In this chapter, we'll be taking a look at two simple examples of collecting contact information – adding a contact form to your blog, and adding a link to an email list on your site. If you're going through hands on, this chapter is based on the previous two chapters – but if you're just reading to learn, it's still a good way to learn about the kinds of things you run into with marketing automation.

At some point, you end up needing to "connect all the dots", and this is an example of connecting systems. It's a simple example, but I'd still recommend trying it out, to get a concrete sense of the "core' of marketing automation, which centers on collecting customer information (so that you can follow up on it).

When you're reading this book, if you're ready to take things to the next level, you're also welcome to schedule a free consultation, to see how Rainmaker Internet Marketing can help your business make use of marketing automation. Please visit rainma.com/automation

Adding a Contact form to a Blog (Blogger)

As you saw in Chapter 4, Blogger is probably the easiest, quickest ways to get a blog going. In this section, we'll take a look at how to add the email list you created in the last chapter, to your Blogger blog.

To begin, you'll probably want to have a couple tabs in your browser open, or separate windows. First we'll go into Mailchimp, and you may want to log into Blogger in a separate tab/window.

Go into MailChimp to Get the List

So, to begin, log into Mailchimp, go to Lists, and on the Lists page, click the downward arrow next to "Stats":

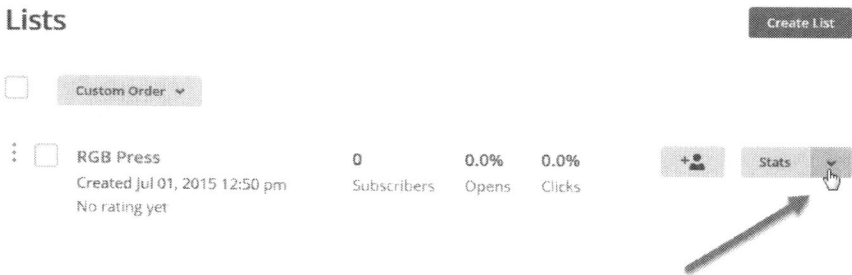

Next, choose the Signup forms option. We're going to get the code for your form that Mailchimp created, so we can take it into Blogger.

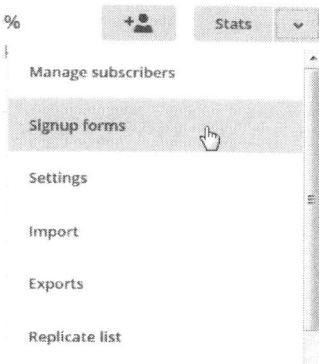

Click the Select button in the Embedded Forms section:

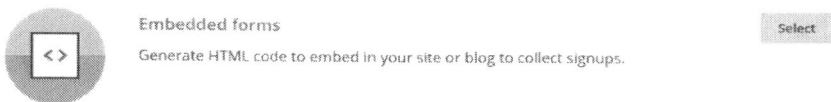

Now, you'll be presented with the Embedded forms window, where you can go back and make adjustments at any time. The window includes a preview of the way the signup form will look.

Embedded forms

| Classic | Super Slim | Naked | Advanced |

The Classic Form includes all visible fields for this list.

Form options

☑ Include form title

    Subscribe to our mailing list

○ Show only required fields
    Edit required fields in the form builder.

◉ Show all fields

Preview

Subscribe to our mailing list

                             * indicates required

Email Address
                                  *

First Name

Last Name

Scroll down towards the bottom, and look for the Copy/paste section:

☑ Show interest group fields

☑ Show required field indicators

☑ Show format options
    HTML, plain-text, mobile options.

Optional: **Form width**

Form width in pixels. Leave blank to let the form take on the width of the area where it's placed.

Copy/paste onto your site

```
<!-- Begin MailChimp Signup Form -->
<link href="//cdn-images.mailchimp.com/embedcode/classic-081711.css" rel="stylesheet" type="text/css">
<style type="text/css">
        #mc_embed_signup{background:#fff; clear:left; font:14px Helvetica,Arial,sans-serif; }
        /* Add your own MailChimp form style overrides in your site stylesheet or in this style block.
```

Next you can just click in the Copy/paste section, to select all the code.

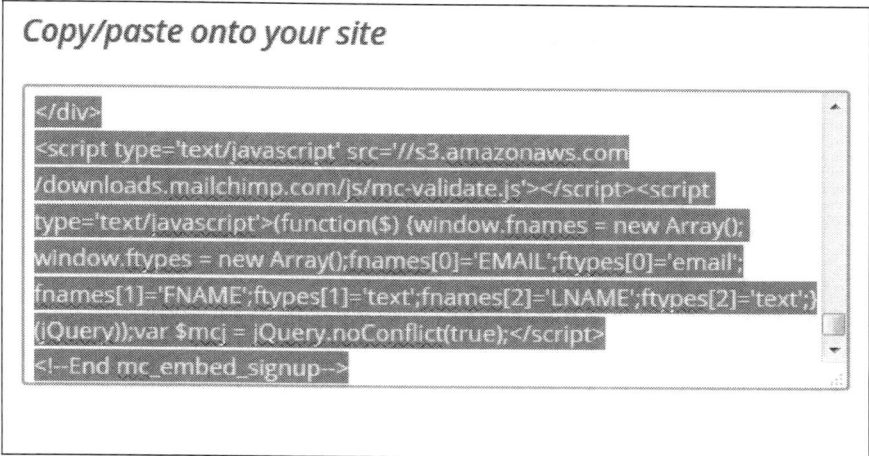

Copy/paste onto your site

```
</div>
<script type='text/javascript' src='//s3.amazonaws.com
/downloads.mailchimp.com/js/mc-validate.js'></script><script
type='text/javascript'>(function($) {window.fnames = new Array();
window.ftypes = new Array();fnames[0]='EMAIL';ftypes[0]='email';
fnames[1]='FNAME';ftypes[1]='text';fnames[2]='LNAME';ftypes[2]='text';}
(jQuery));var $mcj = jQuery.noConflict(true);</script>
<!--End mc_embed_signup-->
```

Next, you can right-click (Windows) or CTRL+click (Mac) and select the Copy option, to copy the code into memory. We're picking up the code here, and we'll drop it into Blogger.

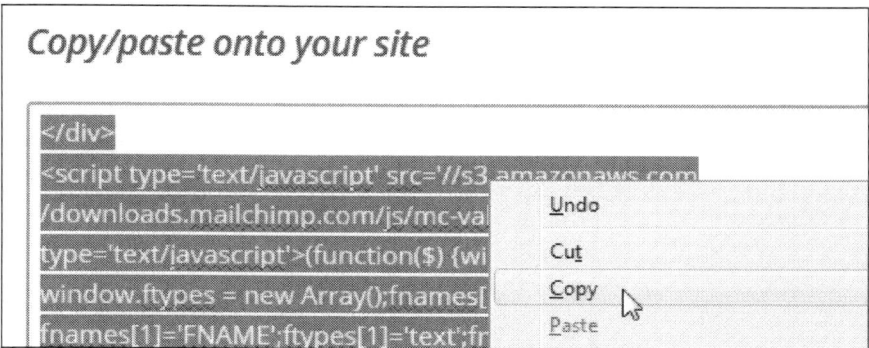

Copy/paste onto your site

```
</div>
<script type='text/javascript' src='//s3.amazonaws.com
/downloads.mailchimp.com/js/mc-va
type='text/javascript'>(function($) {wi
window.ftypes = new Array();fnames[
fnames[1]='FNAME';ftypes[1]='text';fr
```

| Undo |
| Cut |
| Copy |
| Paste |

Get the List into Blogger

Now that you've got the code, log into blogger.com, and select your blog:

Blogger

Todd Kelsey ▾

Todd Kelsey's blogs

English (United States) ▾ ⚙

New Blog

Todd's Marketing Blog

View blog

653 pageviews   11 posts, last published on May 4, 2015

We're going behind the scenes – so look for "Layout" on the left, and select it:

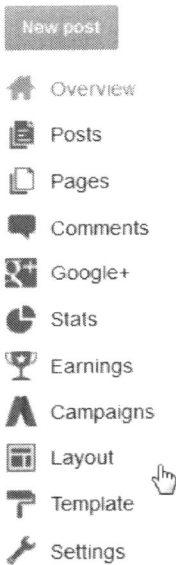

New post

🏠 Overview

📋 Posts

📄 Pages

💬 Comments

Google+

📊 Stats

🏆 Earnings

⚔ Campaigns

📊 Layout

🖌 Template

🔧 Settings

Then, depending on the template you used to make your blog, you will probably have a "sidebar" column. Click the Add a Gadget link. We're going to make a space on the layout for the email list.

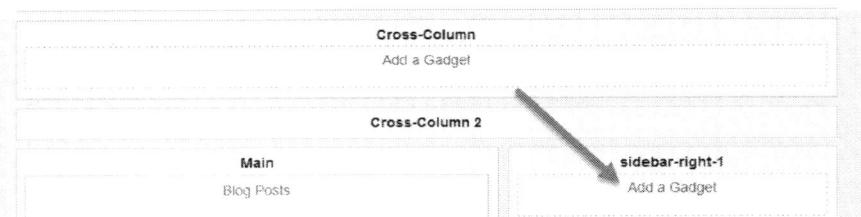

Cross-Column		
Add a Gadget		
Cross-Column 2		
Main		**sidebar-right-1**
Blog Posts		Add a Gadget

In the Gadgets window, scroll down until you see this Gadget, and click the + sign:

HTML/JavaScript
Add third-party functionality or other code to your blog.
By Blogger

The Gadget will open up and look something like this. You can type in a Title like "Email List":

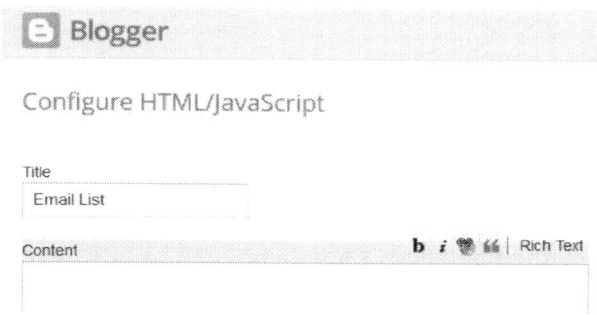

Blogger

Configure HTML/JavaScript

Title
Email List

Content   b *i* 💗 66 | Rich Text

The "Content" section is where you'll be placing the "code", which happens to be HTML/Javascript. Fancy that – now you're a coder!

So click in the Content section, and "paste" the code that you copied over from Mailchimp (ex: CTRL+V)

Content   **b** *i* 🖐 66 | Rich Text

```
      <div class="clear"><input type="submit"
value="Subscribe" name="subscribe" id="mc-embedded-
subscribe" class="button"></div>
      </div>
</form>
</div>
<script type='text/javascript' src='//s3.amazonaws.com
/downloads.mailchimp.com/js/mc-validate.js'></script>
<script type='text/javascript'>(function($) {window.fnames
= new Array(); window.ftypes = new
Array();fnames[0]='EMAIL';ftypes[0]='email';
fnames[1]='FNAME';ftypes[1]='text';fnames[2]='LNAME';
ftypes[2]='text';}(jQuery));var $mcj =
jQuery.noConflict(true);</script>
<!--End mc_embed_signup-->
```

| Save | Cancel | Back |

Then, click the Save button.

And on the blog page, at the top, click the Save arrangement button:

Todd's Marketing Blog · Layout   Save arrangement

In order to see how things look, click the View blog button:

View blog

And in theory, your blog should look something like this:

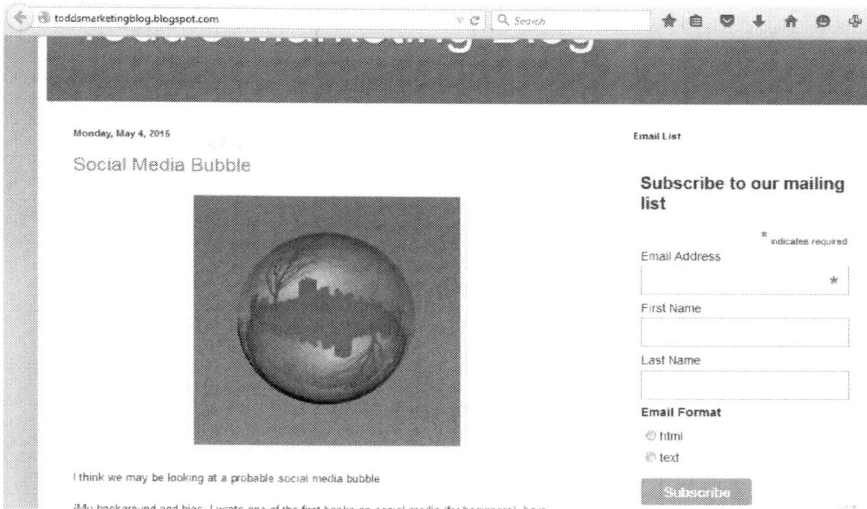

Next, try out the sign-up process!

Adding an email list to a Website (Google Sites)

In this section, we're going to add the link for the email list to the website you created. This is an example of a "workaround". Ideally, a website system or platform would just accept the code like Blogger did, and display a form.

For whatever reason, Google Sites is having issues at the time of writing – its settings are more restricted than Blogger evidently (or Mailchimp's code is not "compliant", or 10 other reasons). The bottom line is, sometimes when integrating systems, you need to do a workaround. (Or, in trying things – you reach a point where a more customizable, flexible platform like Wordpress becomes necessary).

(Note: For those of you exploring various web platforms, your suggested homework is to revisit Chapter 4, look at the end at the various free/low-cost web platforms, and then go through and make a super simple site in each of them, including adding a contact form. Plus, for further extra credit, try creative Googling, such as "mailchimp email lists on weebly", or "adding mailchimp to strikingly", and so on.)

So, log into Google Sites (http://sites.google.com), and select the site you created during Chapter 4:

Google

Search my sites

Sites

CREATE   **CASA Curriculum**   Shared with everyone in the world
           /site/casamktgcurriculum/

Then, either edit an existing page you created (the pencil icon at the top), or click the Create Page icon (next to the pencil):

tekelsey@gmail.com ▾

Create page (c)

Come up with a name (ex: Email List), type it in, and click the Create button:

CREATE   Cancel

Create a page in Site: CASA Curriculum

Name your page:

Your page URL: /site/casamktgcurriculum/ change URL

Next, your site should look something like this, and the cursor will already be placed in the page, ready for you to type information:

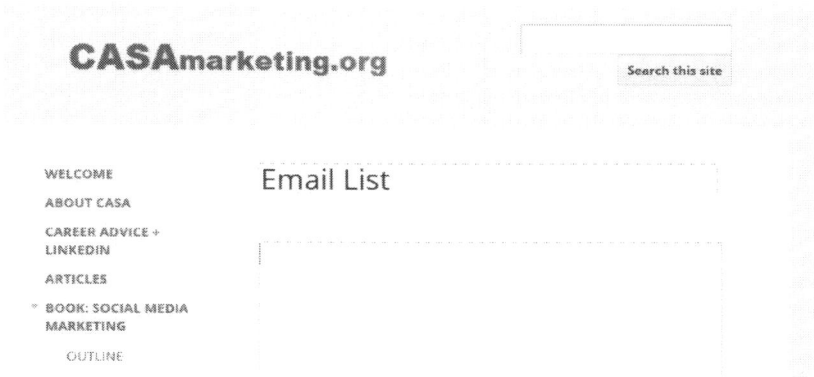

CASAmarketing.org   Search this site

WELCOME   Email List
ABOUT CASA
CAREER ADVICE +
LINKEDIN
ARTICLES
BOOK: SOCIAL MEDIA
MARKETING
OUTLINE

Next, if you don't have it written down somewhere, you'll want to go back into Chapter 5, and follow the instructions for getting the link for your email list, and it should look something like:
http://eepurl.com/br5Gb9

So, copy the link into memory, and come back and type an introductory sentence like the following on the page in Google Sites:

Please click on the link below to join our email list!

Then, click the "chainlink" icon at the top of the typing window, to create a link:

In the "Create Link" window, click on Web address, to tell Google Sites that you want to link to another Web site.

Create Link

Sites page	
Web address	**Site map** My Recent Changes
Apps Script	CASA Curriculum

Then, paste the link for your email list into the Text and Link fields:

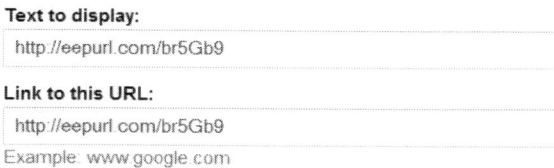

Text to display:

http://eepurl.com/br5Gb9

Link to this URL:

http://eepurl.com/br5Gb9

Example: www.google.com

Then, click the checkbox for "Open this link in a new window", and click the OK button:

Open this link in a new window

OK   Cancel

Finally, be sure to click the Save button at the top, to save the page you're working on.

tekelsey@gmail.com ▾

draft saved at 9:47 AM   Save   Cancel

Then your page should look something like this. Technically, it's nicer to have a form display, based on the idea of always having "one less click" for people to go through – but it works.

CASAmarketing.org

Search this site

WELCOME

ABOUT CASA

CAREER ADVICE +
LINKEDIN

ARTICLES

BOOK: SOCIAL MEDIA
MARKETING

Email List

Please click on the link below to join our email list!

http://eepurl.com/br5Gb9

Congratulations on adding the link to a live Web site!

Don't forget, that until recently, you needed to have significant technical skills to put a website together. You'd have to put all the code together on your computer, upload it, test it. Nowadays, with tools like Google Sites, it does most of the work for you. It's kind of like that with marketing automation. Even if you end up deciding to work with an agency, it may be helpful to explore various tools and their capabilities, so you can "Speak the language", and have a better understanding, and more confidence, to be able to make a good decision. Who knows, you might even have fun! And I can almost guarantee you, *especially* if you feel a sense of intimidation, that if you work through it, it will feel good to do it yourself. Try, ask questions, forge ahead. Woohoo!

Industry Perspective: In the Trenches on Social Media

Caleb Clausen
Marketing Associate
Rainmaker Internet Marketing

Todd: You work at Rainmaker, and help execute some of the outreach on social media, both for Rainmaker and clients. What social networks do you work with?

Caleb: For most of them, it is the "Big 3" - Facebook, Twitter, and Google+. Some are on Pinterest. A few of our clients are also on LinkedIn.

What tools do you use to manage social media? Hootsuite? Was it hard to learn? How did you learn it?

I use Hootsuite to manage almost all of our social media accounts. It is an incredibly useful tool that saves me a tons of time. This frees me up to work on other areas of client accounts. Hootsuite allows me to make a post to all social media platforms for one client at one time, rather than going into each social network and posting separately for each one. Hootsuite was not difficult to learn at all. A coworker taught me and began using it independently shortly after that.

What's your workflow for content?

I generate the content that is posted for all social media accounts. I keep the posts light and relatable, while peppering in some self-promotional stuff for the client and industry-related news. I adhere to the 80/20 rule, where 80% of the content is directed toward the followers/fans, and 20% is self-promotional content for the client.

Once I come up with the content, I go into Hootsuite and select the social accounts for the client I'm posting for. I then paste the content into Hootsuite, and can either post it right at that moment or schedule it to be posted at a later time. You can schedule posts months into the future if you wanted to!

Is it often an ebook of some kind, or general information?

For that 20% of self-promotional content, I use a variety of things. I take blog posts from clients' websites and post them to social media, E-books, other info from their websites, etc.

What's it been link to post on LinkedIn? Do you post to discussion groups?

Posting to LinkedIn is a little different than the other "Big 3". It's a more professional social network. I post to discussion groups occasionally. It's been a learning experience; it requires different kinds of content, more professional -- you're not going to post what you had for breakfast or watch kitten videos. Instead, you're going to connect with potential clients, customers, mentors and referrers. I do a lot of work on LinkedIn for our company (Rainmaker). This work includes joining and participating in LinkedIn groups, which are a great way to connect with other people within your industry. To see some of the material we post on LinkedIn, visit: https://www.linkedin.com/company/838705

Conclusion/Discussion

Congratulations on making it through the sixth chapter, and getting some hands-on experience! We've taken a longer look at how you can fit some of the basic pieces together for marketing automation, and we also got some perspective on how social media can tie in. (Ex: if you have a blog, that's a likely source of content to post to social media). And in the end, no matter how you promote your site, ultimately you want to draw people in, and get their contact information.

At this point it may be helpful to consider, or even try, getting people to sign up for an email list. So you can just have a "sign up" form or link, and if people like what they read, they "might" sign up for it. But the with "Inbound Marketing", and "Marketing Automation", you take this one step further – you intentionally offer something that might be valuable for your audience, and then in *exchange* for contact information, then visitors get to download it. (ex: an ebook).

For an immediate example, see: http://offer.rainma.com/the-30-greatest-lead-generation-tips-tricks-ideas
or: http://tinyurl.com/rainma-ebook (same link)

In the next chapters, we'll take a closer look at Mailchimp, and how to set a simple example of marketing automation in motion.

If you're ready to take things to the next level, you're also welcome to schedule a free consultation, to see how Rainmaker Internet Marketing can help your business make use of marketing automation. Please visit rainma.com/automation

Learning More

Here's some links to get you started.

MailChimp > Adding a signup form to your website
http://kb.mailchimp.com/lists/signup-forms/add-a-signup-form-to-your-website

Blogger > Putting code into your Blog
http://blogger-hints-and-tips.blogspot.com/2010/10/putting-html-code-from-third-party-into.html

For More Information

For a complete list of links and resources, visit rainma.com/book

Chapter 7: Hands-On Automating Customer Follow-Up

Introduction

In this chapter, we'll be walking through a hands-on example of doing basic marketing automation, using the paid version of MailChimp (at time of writing, $10 USD). This follows in line with the previous chapters, where you can try starting a site, an email list, and gather customer contact information. Once those fundamental parts are in place, you can take it up a step with some automation.

When you're reading this book, if you're ready to take things to the next level, you're also welcome to schedule a free consultation, to see how Rainmaker Internet Marketing can help your business make use of marketing automation. Please visit rainma.com/automation

A General Suggestion

One way to think about automation, especially if you're learning about the features that programs have, is not to feel like you need to know every feature. Instead, you can simplify things by thinking about your business, and follow contact information around, and ask – what do you want to do with it, and when do you want to follow up?

It's so easy to get lost in all the options that software programs have – the more powerful, the more options. But it's good to remember that you can step outside it, and let *your* business needs drive *how* you automate.

As Brian Young in Chapter 11 rightly relates, exploring marketing automation is also an opportunity to get a better understanding of how your business works. You have to look at it closer. And when you're looking at tools, or looking at one other tools – the best way to navigate may be not to focus on the tools, but to ask yourself – what do you want to do? What kinds of things *can* you do? And you can continue asking yourself that question.

For example, when you dive into Mailchimp, there are screens with 20 different options. My best advice is, don't worry about – concentrate on the basics, take it easy, explore some of the things that are possible. But the software doesn't have to drive your business. It's just a tool.

Diving In - Setup

So to try out marketing automation in Mailchimp, to review, you'll need to upgrade the free account to a paid version (which at the time of writing is $10 USD). After you've set up your account and tried it out (ideally by working through all the hands-on chapters), then you'll want to click on the Automation link at the top:

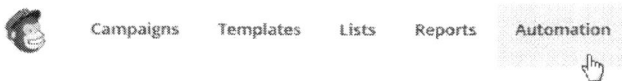

Campaigns   Templates   Lists   Reports   Automation

First, click the Create Automation Workflow button:

≡   Help   Q

Automation   Create Automation Workflow

Next, click the Select A List button (please go back and follow the previous chapters to make an email list if you haven't already). In fact, for testing purposes, you'll probably want to make a new list, only with a couple emails in it.

Which list do you want to use?

Select a list to see workflows.

Select A List ⌄

After you choose a list, you'll get a list of various "workflows" you can try. To start, select Welcome Message:

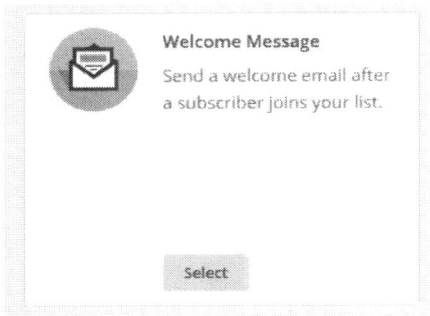

Welcome Message

Send a welcome email after a subscriber joins your list.

Select

In this section, you'll name your workflow – the name doesn't matter particularly much. Mailchimp will "prefill" the "from name" (the name from which the email comes), and the email address it is associated with. You can change those if you like.

Workflow name

Internal use only. Ex: "Newsletter Test#4"

From name   95 characters remaining

NPOEx

Use something subscribers will instantly recognize, like your company name.

From email address

tekelsey@gmail.com

☐ **Send activity digest email**

We'll send you an email every day with a report so you can see how this workflow is performing.

So I'd suggest entering a name like "Welcome", and also clicking on the checkbox to "send activity digest email" so you can get automatic updates when the workflow runs.

Workflow name

| Welcome |

Internal use only. Ex: "Newsletter Test#4"

From name   95 characters remaining

| NPOEx |

Use something subscribers will instantly recognize, like your company name.

From email address

| tekelsey@gmail.com |

☐ Send activity digest email

We'll send you an email every day with a report so you can see how this workflow is performing.

Then, on the same screen, it's worth looking at some of the other features:

☐ **Use Conversations to manage replies**

When enabled, we'll generate a special
reply-to address for your email. We'll filter
"out of office" replies, then thread
conversations into your subscribers'
profiles and display them in reports.

☑ **Personalize the "To:" field**

Include the recipient's name in the
message using merge tags to make it
more personal and help avoid spam
filters. For example, *|FNAME|*
|LNAME| will show "To: Bob Smith" in
the email instead of "To:
bob@example.com". This is more
personal and may help avoid spam filters.

The Personalize feature is worth noting, as an example of the kind of
custom personalization that marketing automation can provide. The
more generic an email is, the less friendly it is – but when you
address people by their name, it comes across better.

Note: See the graphic above for the explanation – this
personalization feature is the "To" in the email itself, in the "header".
Later in the chapter we'll see how you can include personalization in
the body of the email, such as Dear (individual person)"

The way that these features work is, when people sign up for the
email list, Mailchimp can keep track of their name, and
automatically insert it in the email for you.

If you like you can scroll down further on the page to see some of
the options in the Tracking and "More options" sections, but for now
I'd just recommend keeping things as simple as possible, and just
click the Next Step button at the bottom of the page:

Trigger

A "trigger" is a term in marketing automation, which defines a condition for triggering some kind of automated action or sequence. It's very flexible, but you can keep to the basics.

On this screen, it defaults to "when people subscribe".

Configure Trigger

Welcome Message · Change workflow

Trigger workflow when the following conditions are met:

People subscribe to list **NPOEx Newsletter**

Trigger workflow when subscribers are imported
Imported subscribers will **not** be added to this workflow

Add segmentation conditions

Send first email immediately to existing subscribers who meet conditions

There are a few other options – for now I wouldn't worry about them, but it's worth noting the "Segmentation conditions" option.

In the future, whatever system you use, you'll probably want to segment your customers – that is, figure out the different groups of customers you have. It might be an age range, a type of buyer, etc. When you start thinking about these customer groups, then you can start thinking about sending customized messages to them.

But for now, just click the Next step button:

Next step: Emails >

Emails

Now we'll build an email for this workflow. Just click the Add Email button:

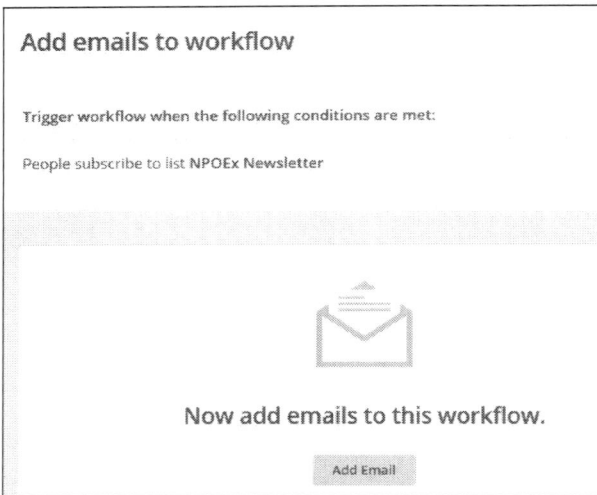

Add emails to workflow

Trigger workflow when the following conditions are met:

People subscribe to list **NPOEx Newsletter**

Now add emails to this workflow.

Add Email

Next you'll get a screen that looks like a timeline, and you'll start to see that you can send more than one email in a workflow sequence. For example, you could have an email 1 day after a person signs up, and then 1 week later. This screen also gives you the ability to design the email; that is, to add content for this particular situation. So, try clicking the Design Email button:

- Trigger workflow when the following conditions are met:

  People subscribe to list **NPOEx Newsletter**

- **1 day after workflow is triggered**
  · Change delay

  | : ✏ ? | **Automation Email #1**
Edited on Jul 08, 2015 11:34 am by you | **Design Email** | 🗑 |

Add Email

You can accept the default email name, or type a new one in. Mailchimp prefills some information, and it can all be customized:

Email Information

Name your email

Automation Email #1

Internal use only. Ex: "Newsletter Test#4"

Email subject   150 characters remaining

☺

How do I write a good subject line? · Emoji support

From name   95 characters remaining

NPOEx

Use something subscribers will instantly recognize, like your company name.

From email address

tekelsey@gmail.com

Next, think of a friendly email subject:

Email subject   120 characters remaining

Welcome to the NPOEx Community   ☺

How do I write a good subject line? • Emoji support

And then click the Next step button:

Next step: Template >

Templates

Templates are an example of a feature that you'll end up using, the more emails you send. Templates allow you to decide some of the basics beforehand, the things that may not change from email to email, such as your logo, and other information. You can create templates elsewhere in Mailchimp and just select it here, or you can customize from scratch. We'll try the scratch method.

On this screen, click the Select button by the "1 Column" template:

Select a Template

Basic   Themes   Saved Templates   Campaigns   Code Your Own

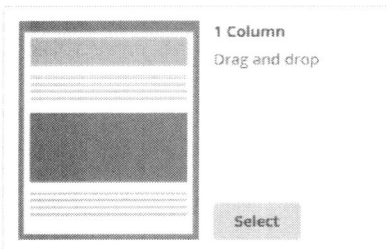

1 Column

Drag and drop

Select

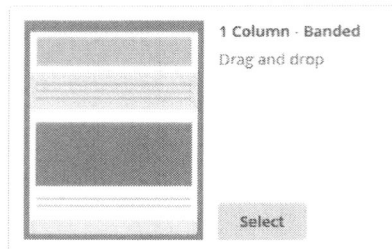

1 Column - Banded

Drag and drop

Select

Next you'll be presented with an editor. You can roll over each section and make changes as desired.

Use this area to offer a short preview of your email's content.   View this email in your browser

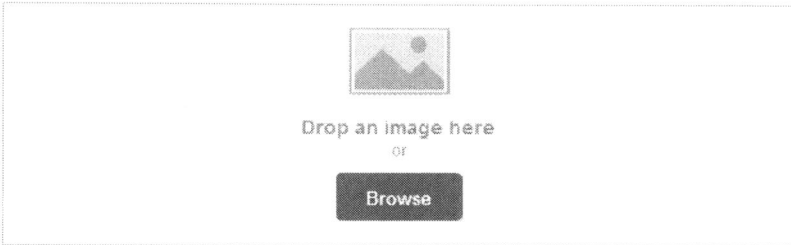

Drop an image here

or

Browse

Designing Your Email

Creating an elegant email is simple

Now that you've selected a template to work with, drag in content blocks to define the structure of your message. Don't worry, you can always delete or rearrange blocks as needed. Then click "Design" to define fonts, colors, and styles.

Need inspiration for your design? Here's what other MailChimp users are doing.

Try taking a graphic on your computer and dragging it onto the top part of the editor:

Use this area to offer a short preview of your email's content.   View this email in your browser

NPOEx

Designing Your Email

Creating an elegant email is simple

Now that you've selected a template to work with, drag in content blocks to define the structure of your message. Don't worry, you can always delete or rearrange blocks as needed. Then click "Design" to define fonts, colors, and styles.

Need inspiration for your design? Here's what other MailChimp users are doing.

Getting your logo in an email is as easy as that.

Then notice the top left area – if you don't change this "Use this" content, it will stay as it is and look dumb when you send an email out. (::raises hand::)

Use this area to offer a short preview of your email's content   View this email in your browser

To edit the top area, roll over it with the mouse and click the little pencil icon:

Next, a pop-out window will appear where you can edit the text.

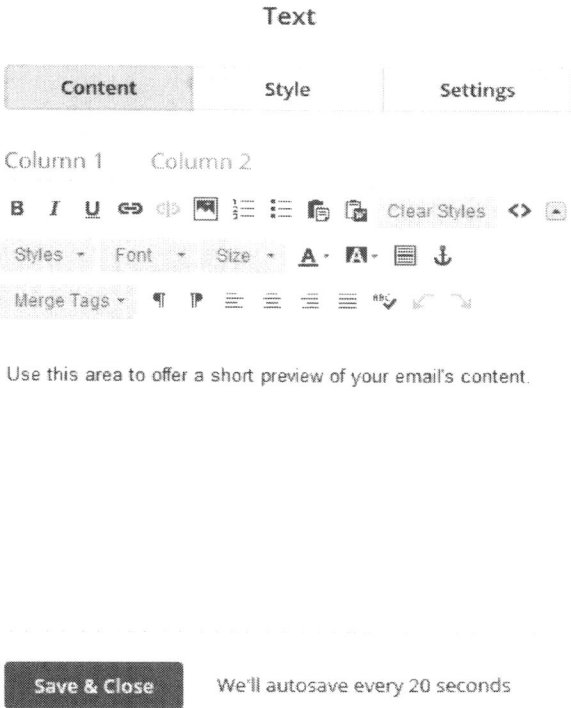

Make changes as desired, then click the Save & Close button.

And you'll see the change reflect at the top.

The rest is as simple. Roll over the section desired, click the pencil icon, and make changes:

And you'll end up with something like this:

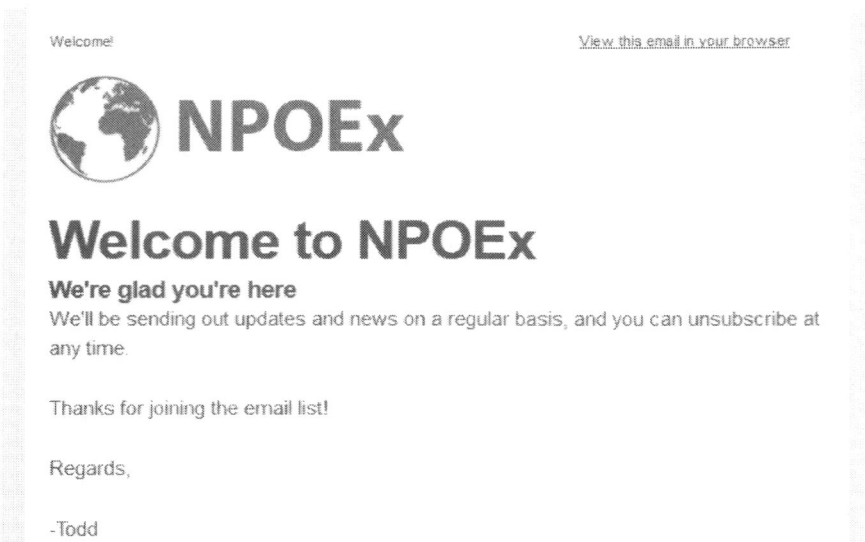

Jedi Powers in Mailchimp

While you're at it, if you're editing the text of the body of the email, you can make use of your Jedi powers and personalize the greeting. If you like, try placing the cursor at the beginning of the email, and clicking the little Merge Tags drop-down menu:

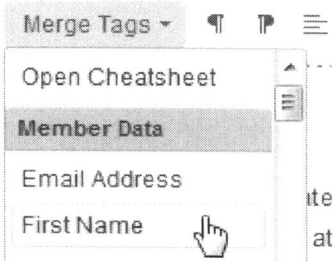

Then you could type in "Dear" before the little code it places in there:

Dear *|FNAME|*

We'll be sending out updates and news on a regular basis, and you can unsubscribe at any time.

This is an example of having the right code, which will automatically pull in the right name, and make things more personalized. As if you were personally writing each email. When you're ready, click the Finish button:

And you'll be brought back to the workflow screen.

Add emails to workflow

- **Trigger workflow when the following conditions are met:**

  People subscribe to list **NPOEx Newsletter**

- **1 day after workflow is triggered**
  · Change delay

  ⋮ ✎ ▢ Automation Email #1 [Edit ▾] 🗑
  Edited on Jul 08, 2015 11:44 am by
  you

Now, click the Next step button:

[Next step: Confirm ›]

And you'll be "ready to send", which means you'll set up the automated workflow, so that whenever the conditions are met (ex: someone signing up), Mailchimp will automatically send an email, instead of you having to send an email yourself.

Ready to send. Review your workflow:

List
You will be sending to "NPOEx Newsletter".
[Edit]

Tracking
You chose to track clicks and opens in the HTML email and clicks in the plain-text email.
[Edit]

Email Authentication
Automatic email authentication will be enabled for this message.
[Edit]

Trigger workflow when the following conditions are met
People subscribe to list NPOEx Newsletter
[Edit]

When you're ready to go, click the Start Workflow button:

Start Workflow

If you're just testing things out, then the next step would be to go ahead and sign up for the email list, or asking a friend to. If you're already on the list and have only one email you can use, try going into the list, deleting your email from it, signing up, and waiting a day to see what happens.

Getting Help

At this point it's a good time to remember if you come across any features or terms you want to understand better, you can visit the Help section on Mailchimp's site: http://kb.mailchimp.com

You can search for specific items at the top, and there's also "pre-fab" items down at the bottom that you might like to explore. And if you run into trouble that the resources don't solve, you can email Mailchimp at help@mailchimp.com

Exploring Segments – VIPs

As you learn more about marketing automation, there are a variety of ways that you can segment customers to have particular messages sent to them, based on particular conditions.

The reason you segment your customers, is so that they get the right message, at the right time. Such as a thank you, or a special offer, etc. And you may end up having different groups of customers, such as good customers, high-value customers, lapsed customers, or just different age groups or types.

In some cases, with some systems, you might manually "tag" someone into a particular customer group. Or you might end up having a system automatically "tag" a customer, if they filled out a form, and chose something like, "I'm ready to buy", or "just doing research", etc.

In this section, we'll take a simple approach, with a "pre-fab" category Mailchimp has, called "VIPs".

TIP: If you explore this, try test on a small "test" email list. Have two people join, or join yourself with two different email addresses.

So, you might want to go to the help center mentioned in the previous section, and try looking up "segments", or in this case, "VIP":

Designate and Send to VIP Subscribers

Mark important subscribers as **VIPs** in your MailChimp account to send targeted campaigns using segmenting conditions, and use MailChimp **VIPs** for iOS or Android t ...

Lists : Manage Subscribers · Jun 17, 2015

http://kb.mailchimp.com/lists/managing-subscribers/designate-and-send-to-vip-subscribers

In the article, it talks about how to mark people as VIPs.

> Follow the steps below to designate subscribers as VIPs.
>
> 1. Navigate to the *Lists* page.
>
> 2. Click the title of the list you want to work with.
>
> 3. Use the checkboxes to select the subscribers you want to designate as VIPs.
>
> 4. Click the *Actions* drop-down menu and select *VIP*.
>
> 5. Select *Add* to mark the subscribers you've checked as VIPs.

For example, you could go into Lists, select a list:

Campaigns   Templates   Lists   Reports   Automation

Then you might select individuals who are VIPs that you want to send special emails to from time to time:

	Email
☐	lpelleg
☐	eric.m
☐	jimmy
☐	radius

And then in the action menu you select VIP:

And then the Add option:

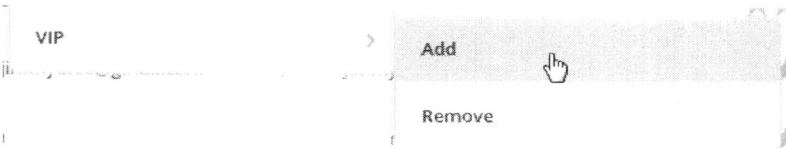

And that kind of process is an example of "segmenting". If you go back to the beginning of the chapter, in the screen where you create a workflow and you can have a "Segmentation" condition, this is where a segment like VIP comes into play. By marking/tagging/designating individual people as a customer segment, then you can send special emails to that segment.

Translated into another way, you might have "everyday" customers, and a group of high-value important customers called VIPs. You might send a special offer to the VIPs, and a different offer to the everyday customers. And marketing automation systems can help you with that.

NOTE: Regarding Mailchimp Free vs Automation

So for anyone exploring Mailchimp, technically there's some automation in the free version. It doesn't have workflows per se, but technically, in the Subscribe forms, you can customize and activate a "final welcome email"

Subscribe
  Signup form
  Signup form with alerts
  Signup "thank you" page
  Opt-in confirmation email
  Opt-in confirmation captcha
  Confirmation "thank you" page
  Final "welcome" email

Unsubscribe
  Unsubscribe form
  Unsubscribe success page
  "Goodbye" email

Update Profile
  Profile update email
  Profile update email sent
  Update profile form
  Update profile sample form
  Update profile "thank you" page

Signup form

So if that's all you want to do, the free version may be fine for you. But as soon as you want to segment groups, or personalize things further, that's when you get into more sophisticated automation, requiring the paid version.

Exploring Additional Tools

One of the things I remember when I was teaching at a Community college, and serving on a special Advisory council, is a member of the council from another college that had a good approach in the field of editing video. So their students would come in, and there were various kinds of platforms and tools that they could learn in different classes. And what this school tried to emphasize is that it's not about the tool, it's about learning the best practices that apply regardless of the tool you're using. So it helped students be competitive, because they weren't locked into a particular tool.

So I think it's helpful to consider your business apart from individual systems, and also to look at some of the features and value propositions that different systems have.

The field is always changing – companies merge, are always adding new features. Case in point, in reading a recent article in techcrunch.com, the writer discussed some startups circa Summer 2015, who are in the marketing automation space, and orienting themselves around small businesses.

I encourage you to try taking a look at some of these startup tools, to see how they communicate the value of marketing automation, and some of the tools they have. Some of them are more mature companies than others.

http://www.nimble.com
https://www.insightly.com/
https://www.pipedrive.com/
https://getbase.com/
https://www.nutshell.com/

Remember to keep on exploring – hire some help if you need to, but the more you're willing to scratch the surface, the better decision you'll make. And remember to think about your own business. You don't need to build your business around options in a software program – you need to build it around your customers.

Conclusion/Discussion

Congratulations on making it through the last hands on chapter, and getting some concrete experience!

Frankly, you've achieved a lot – you've created a website, started an email list, set in motion various ways to capture customer information, and then explored how to automate follow up. Pretty sophisticated stuff! And if you don't believe me that tools these days make life so much easier, try going back and doing all this manually: get yourself a web hosting account, use dreamweaver to make your website, make a form for contact information, and then connect it to a database. Try using outlook (not webmail) to manage all your contacts, or keep them in an Excel file. Then try using calendar reminders as individual inquiries come in. And then pretty soon you'll have a deep appreciation for the time you can save with even basic basic marketing automation.

And the point is, marketing automation can not only help you grow your business, but develop more sophisticated follow up as your business grows. In the next chapter, we'll take another look at Infusionsoft, a little deeper this time, to see what more sophisticated marketing automation looks like.

If you're ready to take things to the next level, you're also welcome to schedule a free consultation, to see how Rainmaker Internet Marketing can help your business make use of marketing automation. Please visit rainma.com/automation

Learning More

Here's some links to get you started.

Mailchimp's Help area has a lot of good resources:
http://kb.mailchimp.com

Try looking at the "VIP" article to learn about segmenting:

http://kb.mailchimp.com/lists/managing-subscribers/designate-and-send-to-vip-subscribers

And you might want to watch this Mailchimp workflows video, or watch it again:
https://www.youtube.com/watch?v=NuftV4sp99M

For More Information

For a complete list of links and resources, visit rainma.com/book

Chapter 8: Lead Nurturing with Infusionsoft

Introduction

In this chapter, we'll be taking a look at the nuts and bolts of how a simple lead nurturing campaign comes together in Infusionsoft. At the time of writing, Infusionsoft doesn't have a free trial available, but in some cases, when you are engaging a sales rep, they "might" be able to give you a limited demo. Either way, it's helpful to look at some of the possibilities that marketing automation has, how it works under the hood, and perhaps most importantly, the part that is independent of any particular tool – the processes that it can help strengthen and automate for your business.

When you're reading this book, if you're ready to take things to the next level, you're also welcome to schedule a free consultation, to see how Rainmaker Internet Marketing can help your business make use of marketing automation. Please visit <u>rainma.com/automation</u>

Infusionsoft Campaign Builder

First, we'll look at how Infusionsoft "wraps" marketing automation capability, within their overall, integrated system. In Infusionsoft's case, you log in to an overall dashboard:

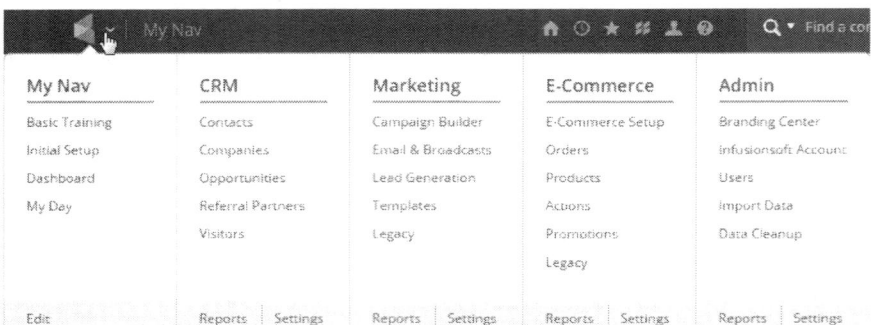

And then within the Marketing section, you access the Campaign builder.

Marketing

Campaign Builder

Email & Broadcasts

Lead Generation

Templates

Legacy

Starting a new campaign is as simple as clicking the Create a Campaign button:

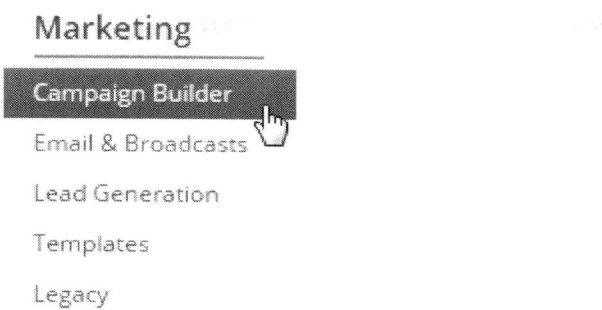

And when you open up the campaign, you are presented with a workspace to create and edit your workflow.

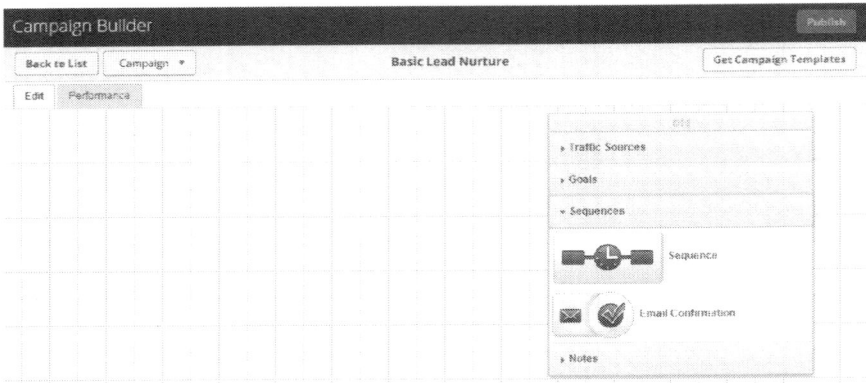

Infusionsoft uses a visual approach, like a visual map of how you want things to work. When I first started looking into sophisticated systems, I was intimidated – all the thousand different options seemed too complex to handle. But gradually, if you flip everything around and base your learning on *scenarios*, it's easier.

So instead of looking at a screen like this and then closing the window and running away in horror (::raises hand::), you can think of Infusionsoft and other systems as tools for your business:

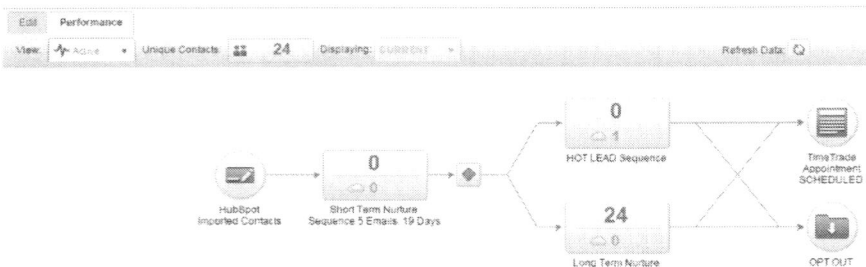

When you think of scenarios, and talk to your customers (ex: see the case study chapter about Brian Young), then you can start to think about what ways you'd like to follow up with customers, *apart from any individual system*, and that will help you to bring it into a system, and work with it. For example, the above graphic may look foreign, but basically it's a high level map of following up with customers – they've downloaded an ebook, and there's a sequence of emails that are sent to them. There's a "nurture" sequence that attempts to offer them something of value, as well as inviting them to make an appointment. And under the right conditions, if they decide to act on that offer, they might become a "hot lead", and might book an appointment.

So the purpose of the graphic above is to show the high-level of the campaign – but in concrete terms, it's meant to work towards getting someone to make an appointment for a phone call. So in the diagram, you also see that it is on the "performance" tab. So when the campaign is running, the stages show how many people have reached a particular stage. For example, if you click on the long term nurture sequence with the 24 on it, it reveals the "entire" sequence. And because it is showing performance, it shows how many people are at a particular stage.

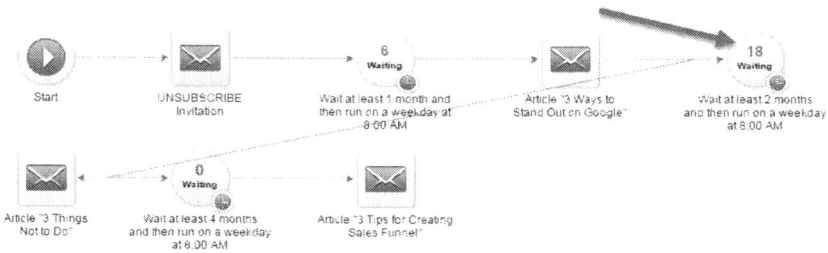

So basically, the idea is that you can plan a sophisticated, automated sequence of various emails, and then you can see how many people get to particular "Stages".

For example, when you're reviewing a live campaign, you can see exactly who is at a particular stage:

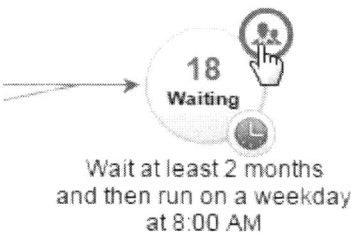

And then view this list of people in the Contacts area:

⊷⊟ Campaign Contacts Waiting (back to campaign)

✔	1-18 of 18
✔	Name
✔	Terras:
✔	David I
✔	Chris
✔	Susan
✔	Julie Fr

So the bottom line of this last section is to show that the simple scenario is, there is a desired to follow up with people who download an ebook, and then the goal is to invite them into booking an actual appointment to discuss services. Some people may call with the first ad. Some people may never call – but in between, there are people who *might* respond, if you provide the right follow up, the right value, at the right time.

Creating a New Lead Sequence

In this section we're going to explore how you can make use of previously-created campaigns in Infusionsoft. In other words, you don't have to necessarily make a campaign from scratch. It's also a great learning experience.

In Infusionsoft, in the Campaign Builder, you click on Get Campaign Templates:

And then you can sort the many templates based on what are most popular:

And you might choose a template like "Free Report" campaign.

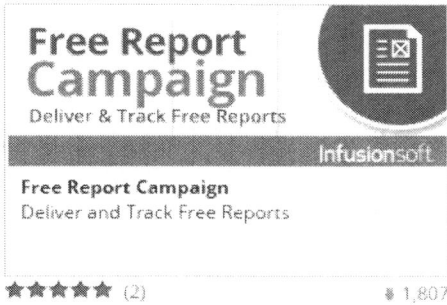

Then, to install it, you just roll over and click Install:

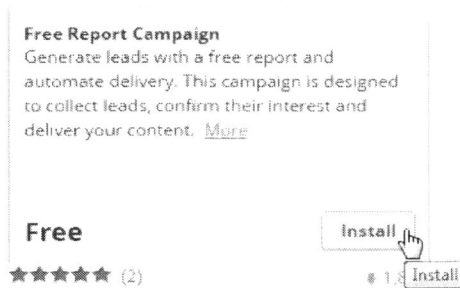

And then the system automatically installs a template that you can further customize:

In many cases there are instructions and tips built right into the campaign:

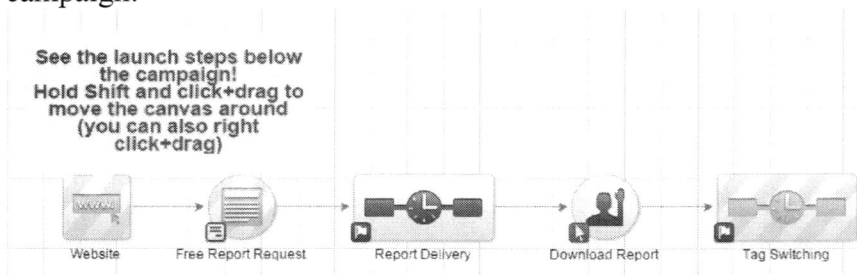

In this campaign, traffic comes from a website, and the sequence of events is for people to request a report, receive an email, and then ideally actually download the report. There's no "one way" of doing things, it's just an example we'll follow to see how things work in Infusionsoft.

So if we took a look at the first section, which is also called a "goal" we can see there are a number of options, when you click on the little "sub icon" in the lower left, which allows you to adjust the goal settings:

Free Report Request

The window opens up, and the goals can be set to a variety of actions, such as the goal of someone submitting a web form, clicking a particular link, purchasing a product, etc:

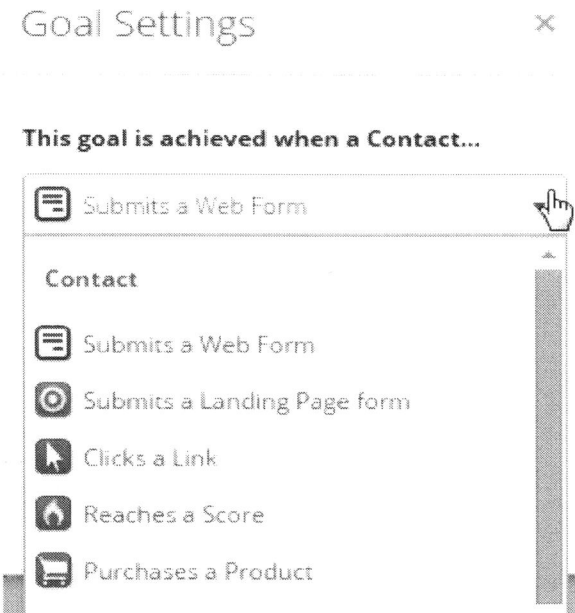

The goal in Infusionsoft is basically a statement of where you want people to go – and then if they reach that goal, you can have things automatically happen. So if we go back and double click on the overall icon, and double-click on it, it allows you to edit/adjust the specific goal you've chosen (in this case, submitting a Web form)

And this is where you start to see some of the power of marketing automation. So if you start back at square one and ask yourself how you might *manually* accomplish all the customer follow-up, it is probably a good exercise, and many businesses are doing just that: they get emails or calls, make a note of them somewhere, on paper, wherever, put some of them into an excel spreadsheet, and then maybe go so far as to set a calendar reminder of when to follow up. But of course, that system could rapidly break down.

Then, the next stage might be trying to manually put together a bunch of website related tools – such as an email tool, making a web form, etc. – and then trying to automate it somehow.

But in Infusionsoft, you can access most or all of the functions all in one tool. For example, when you open up the web form Goal, it opens up a live, editable web form.

When you're using a pre-created template, it may have some instructions in there to walk you through things, but basically what you're looking at is an email editor. In other words, as part of marketing automation, when you need a particular thing, you can plan it at a high-level, visually, as we saw in the previous step, and then click on things to edit them, like a web form, below:

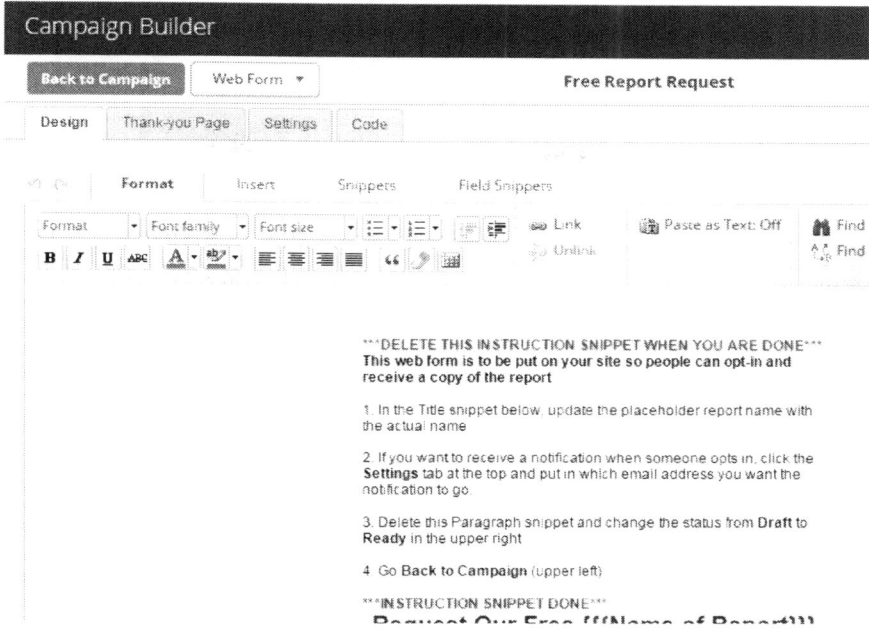

And when you scroll down in the editing window you see something like this:

Request Our Free {{{Name of Report}}} Report!

First Name *

Email *

[Email Me A Copy!]

Now, just for the sake of conversation, if you had to manually build a form like that, even a simple one, in HTML, it would take some time and technical expertise. You'd have to have a hosting account, then make the code, then upload it, then connect it to a database and script, and configure it, etc. etc.

But the power of the marketing automation system is that it makes it a lot easier, just open it up and start making changes.

Also, in the interface it's helpful to see that there are as many options as you'd want to customize – such as the thank you page that can come after the form, the overall settings, and then code-related options:

And if you click on the Code tab, you'll see that if you want, you can get code for a web developer (or yourself!) to copy and past into a pre-existing web page. But you can also click on "use the hosted version":

And then what you end up with is a simple link, so all you need to do to have a link to the web form is to place it in an email, on a social media post, in a blog post, or on a web page, and it leads to that form (ex: yes I want to get the ebook, here's my contact info):

So Infusionsoft can not only make it easy to create the form, but also give you a central place for managing it, and can put it automatically on the web for you.

And when you go to one the links, you can see your form:

← → C 🔒 https://pw101.infusionsoft.com/app/form/na1071

DELETE THIS INSTRUCTION SNIPPET WHEN YOU ARE DONE
This web form is to be put on your site so people can opt-in and receive a copy of the report

1. In the Title snippet below, update the placeholder report name with the actual name

2. If you want to receive a notification when someone opts in, click the **Settings** tab at the top and put in which email address you want the notification to go.

3. Delete this Paragraph snippet and change the status from **Draft** to **Ready** in the upper right

4. Go **Back to Campaign** (upper left)

INSTRUCTION SNIPPET DONE

Request Our Free {{{Name of Report}}} Report!

First Name *

Email *

Email Me A Copy!

And if you go back into the email editor and take out all the fluff, you can save, re-publish it, and voila! Your form:

🔒 https://pw101.infusionsoft.com/app/form/na1071 ☆

Request Our Free Report!

First Name *

Email *

Email Me A Copy!

So the general overall purpose of this section is just to show how you can plan your overall sequence of events, and then work directly on each moving part, such as a web form.

Delivery Sequence

Next in the sequence comes report delivery. There's more than one approach, and in some cases, you might end up having someone download an ebook from a link, but in this case, the sequence goes to an email that offers a link for download.

In the campaign builder, at a high level, you see the sequence we've been working on, and if you want to look at Report Delivery in more detail, you can double-click on it:

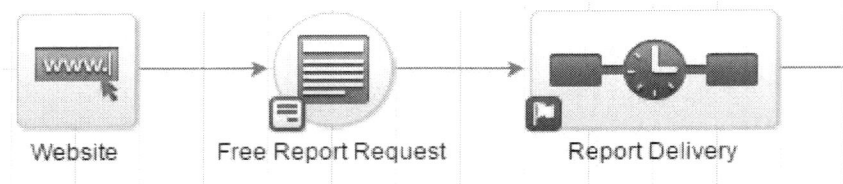

Website   Free Report Request   Report Delivery

Then, a variety of things can happen in a sequence. Earlier in the chapter you saw a more complex sequence – in this case, it's just applying a tag, and sending an email with the report.

Start   Apply 1 tag   Report Delivery

Tags are a feature worth noting as well. To remember and get out of "Abstract Land", what we're talking about is how to communicate with real live customers, and how to keep track of interactions. So if you were doing things all by phone, you might have a 3x5 card with the new prospect's name, and if they requested that you mail them a report, you might mark it down on a card, to remind yourself that this customer requested information. That means they might be interested.

So a tag is the system's way of doing the same thing. "This person requested a report".

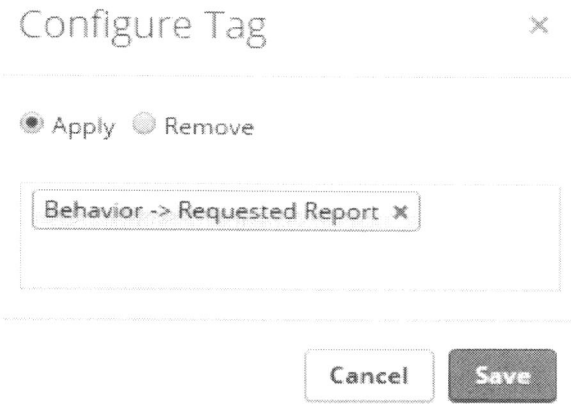

Configure Tag   ×

◉ Apply   ○ Remove

Behavior -> Requested Report ×

Cancel   Save

And of course tags are customizable.

Next, in our sequence, there's the email itself.

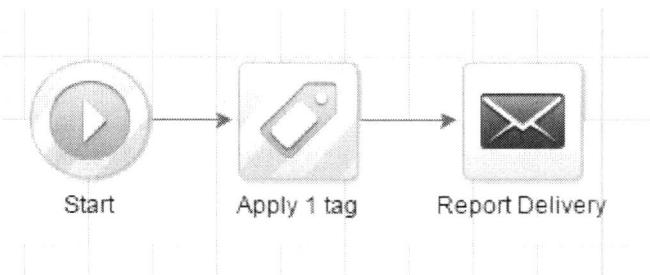

Start   Apply 1 tag   Report Delivery

Emails, like web forms, are also editable, right in the system. You can customize the template as much as you like, and the system will automatically send the email, insert personalized info, just at the time you choose.

In the visual Campaign Builder, you can double click on the Report Delivery icon (which represents an email), and edit the template directly:

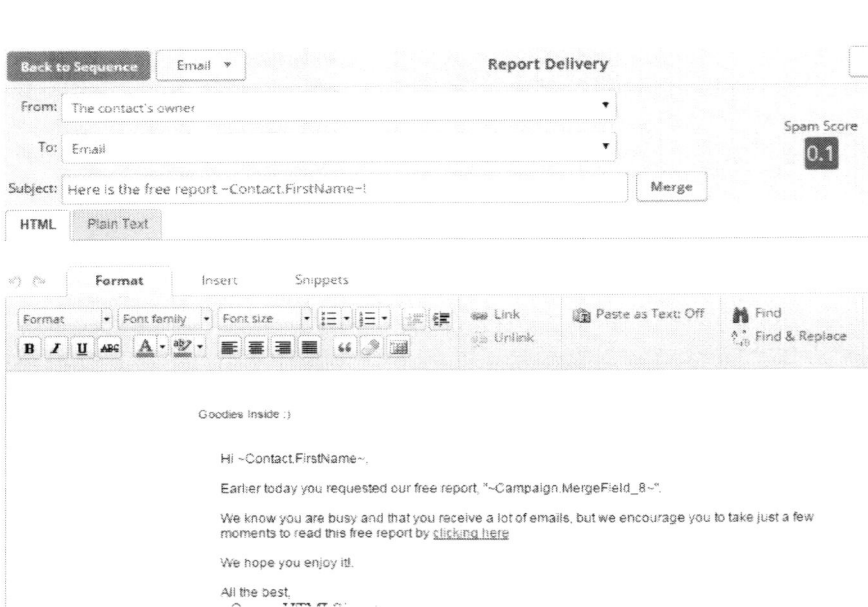

Download Goal

Now we're going back out to the high-level view in the campaign, where we see our overall sequence, starting with the source of traffic, following with the web form (free report request), and continuing with the Report Delivery (which is where a tag was applied, and an email sent). Next, we look at the ultimate goal in this campaign, which is to get someone to actually download the report.

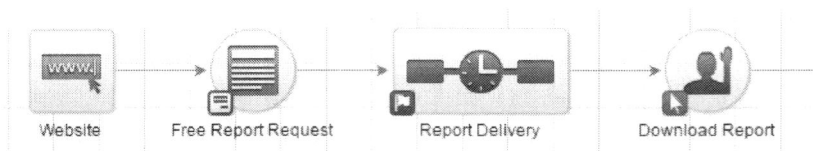

So in the Campaign Builder, if we click on the Goal Settings icon in the lower left-hand corner of the goal icon (the little blue arrow in this case), we can see the Goal settings. Compare this to the diagram earlier in the chapter, of the goal settings for a Web form. We're just saying, ok, at this point our goal is to have people click on a particular link in the email, in order to download the report.

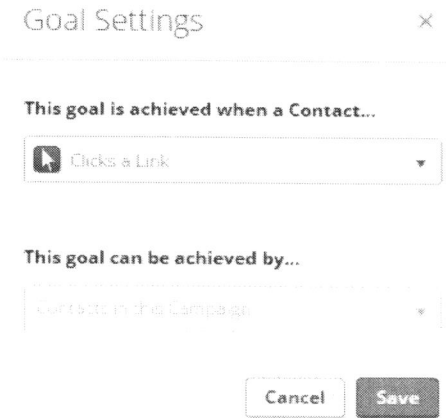

Goal Settings   ✕

This goal is achieved when a Contact...

Clicks a Link   ▾

This goal can be achieved by...

Contacts in the Campaign   ▾

Cancel   Save

And the reason we want to keep track of this is to be able to see who *actually* download the report. That's an important thing with marketing automation – keeping track of who did what, and when.

Next, if you go in and click on the goal itself, this is where you tell the system, "Ok, my goal is after I send this email out, I want you to tell me if they click on this particular link":

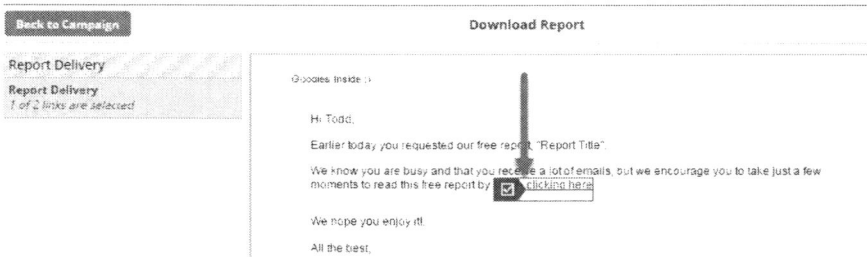

Back to Campaign   Download Report

Report Delivery

Report Delivery
1 of 2 links are selected

Goodies Inside :)

Hi Todd,

Earlier today you requested our free report, "Report Title".

We know you are busy and that you receive a lot of emails, but we encourage you to take just a few moments to read this free report by ☑ clicking here

We hope you enjoy it!

All the best,

And this view is showing a preview of the email – the purpose is not to edit the email itself, but it's to tell the system, "this is what I want to keep track of".

Tag Switching

Next, we are looking at our "full" sample sequence. Someone's filled out the form, they got the email, and if they actually download the report, we want to know. (i.e. "tag switching"). Basically like a game of tag. A customer downloads the report? Tag, you're it!

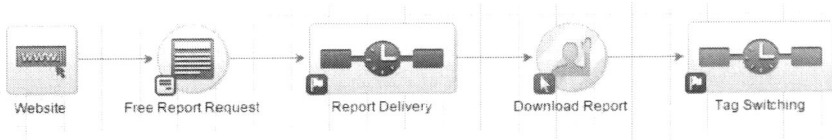

| Website | Free Report Request | Report Delivery | Download Report | Tag Switching |

And if you look closely at the "tag" sequence, a tag is applied.

| Start | Remove 1 tag | Apply 1 tag |

And like the previous tag we looked at, the tag is saying "this person did something". In this case, they downloaded the report.

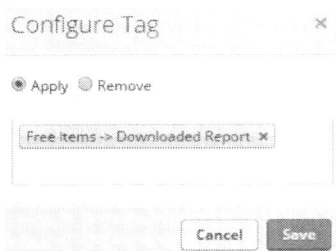

Configure Tag ×

● Apply ○ Remove

Free Items -> Downloaded Report ×

Cancel Save

Sequence Summary

So in these sections, we've been looking at how you can take an important task like customer follow up, and carefully have the system reach out to customers, including if they take particular actions. And once it is set in motion, it happens in the background, and can happen continuously.

So not everyone is likely to reach the "end" of your nurture sequence – but as you work on it, you can increase the number who do, including by actually talking to people, and asking things like "what's the right amount of time to wait before checking in? Are there any more resources we could offer in the meantime that might be helpful? Was the language of the email right?".

And as you can see, you can work visually, to basically diagram your business. You might be evolving your business, but at first, it might just be starting to ask yourself questions like "how do I collect information?", "where does it go?", and "when do I follow up?". Then you can start with a high-level visual diagram, which is not just a visual for marketing automation, but is also giving you a view of your business. And then you can expand it, test it, see what's right for you, both for attracting new customers, and retaining existing customers.

Conclusion/Discussion

Congratulations on making it through this chapter, and getting deeper into the marketing automation experience. I do believe the more that you try it out, ask questions, and approach it with a sense of exploration, the easier it will go. And if you remember one thing from this chapter, I suggest remembering that you can begin without a system – in other words, instead of trying to understand all the features and options of a system, instead you can start simple, and grow from there. Start outside the system, imagine a scenario. Try something like a pre-built template. Make it as simple as possible, so you can get to testing it quickly. Then try it.

One of the things that was most fun for me when trying the system was making a really simple sequence, and then trying it out, filling out the form, getting the email, downloading an ebook, etc. – when you see it live, it comes alive, and it gives you more confidence. And it can help inspire you to, to see how things can come together. Best wishes!

If you're ready to take things to the next level, you're also welcome to schedule a free consultation, to see how Rainmaker Internet Marketing can help your business make use of marketing automation. Please visit rainma.com/automation

Learning More

Here's some links to get you started.

Lifecycle ebook
http://www.infusionsoft.com/resources/ebook/marketing-plan-for-small-business
> an ebook from Infusionsoft that talks about developing a marketing plan for a small business.

Introduction to Lead Nurturing
https://www.act-on.com/whitepaper/introduction-to-lead-nurturing/
> This guide might be helpful in getting your head around actually planning a lead nurturing sequence. It is provided by a "peer" to Infusionsoft and HubSpot, which pricing-wise, sits somewhere in between them.

> *Lead nurturing is the process B2B marketers use to build relationships with these prospects – even when they're not yet ready to buy – in order to win their business when they are ready to buy. Your job as a marketer is to give these prospects the information they need to make a buying*

decision, to keep your brand front-and-center during this period, and to be there when they're finally ready to commit.

In the following guide, we'll explain the six foundational steps your company can take to set up a successful lead nurturing program. These include:

- *Understanding the fundamentals of lead nurturing;*
- *Designing a basic lead nurturing program;*
- *Learning how to refine and expand your program;*
- *Measure the progress of your lead nurturing program; and*
- *Learning how to use lead nurturing to build a better, more productive relationship between your marketing and sales teams.*

--

https://www.act-on.com/about-us/kudos/analyst-acclaim/
> This is some standard showcasey markety stuff, testimonials. If you want to understand the systems, including how some of the more affordable systems like Infusionsoft compare to higher end ones like Marketo, etc., if you go to this link, the Forrester Q1 2014 report is probably good. Q1 of 2014 is already 18 months before the time of writing, and things always change, but it still might help you to have a sense of place.

--

Companies that excel at lead nurturing generate 50% more sales ready leads at 33% lower cost.

So you'll see this stat from a variety of sources if you Google it, and it originally comes from Forrester research, but various marketing automation platforms will quote it. But it's probably worth printing out and taping on the wall. http://www.pardot.com/lead-nurturing/4-major-benefits-nurturing-leads/ (surprise surprise, Pardot also has a guide to offer you)

For More Information

For a complete list of links and resources, visit <u>rainma.com/book</u>

Chapter 9: Lead Nurturing with HubSpot

Introduction

In this chapter, we'll be taking a look at the HubSpot platform, a very popular marketing automation platform, which is worth exploring. HubSpot also has excellent, free training for anyone, and it can be a good way to get a better sense of how marketing automation works, as well as some of the best practices. They've got it "right", as far as how content supports marketing.

When you're reading this book, if you're ready to take things to the next level, you're also welcome to schedule a free consultation, to see how Rainmaker Internet Marketing can help your business make use of marketing automation. Please visit rainma.com/automation

Getting Help

Before you do anything, I'd recommend visiting this link, and bookmarking it:

http://help.hubspot.com/support

When you're trying marketing automation out, it can make your life easier if you make a plan of contact support as soon as you run into any roadblocks.

What I'd recommend doing is making a free trial account, and then come back and access the HELP link, log in if you need to, and make a note of the phone number you need to call (and your HubSpot ID). I guarantee you will be glad you did, in case you end up with any technical issues, or just would like someone to explain features or concepts that are new to you.

Free Training

The next thing I'd recommend, even before opening up a free trial of HubSpot, is exploring their certification program. You don't need to get certified, but it happens to be an excellent course that can help you understand the overall principles of Inbound Marketing, and the ideas behind attracting people with content to help generate sales.

http://academy.hubspot.com/certification
I have students in Content/SEO classes that I teach, do HubSpot certification as part of the learning process; I find the quality to be good. There's videos, additional resources you can download. So you might want to dive in, as you fire up your HubSpot trial.

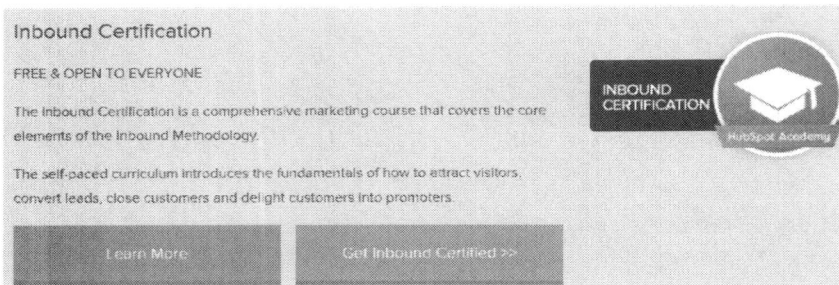

When you have your trial, another way you can get to the material is within HubSpot, up at the right corner, there's a little "graduation hat" icon, and you can choose the Certifications menu.

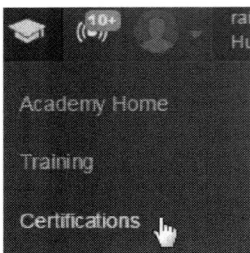

Then, there's a series of videos you can watch:

The Inbound Certification is made up of twelve classes that you can watch on demand and at your own pace. To help you master the topic, each class includes additional resources that dig further into the topic, a self-check quiz, and a transcript of each video if you prefer to read along.

And every class has good material that can help you understand all the "moving pieces"

The Classes

Inbound Fundamentals

✿ Essentials of an Effective Inbound Strategy

Attract

🔍 Optimizing Your Website for Search Engines

📖 Creating Content with a Purpose

📖 The Fundamentals of Blogging

💬 Amplifying Your Content with Social Media

Convert

🔍 Enticing Clicks with Calls-to-Action

📖 The Anatomy of a Landing Page

🔖 Guiding the Next Step with Thank You Pages

Close

✉ Sending the Right Email to the Right Person

⚡ The Power of Smarketing

⚙ Taking Your Sales Process Inbound

...xample, in the first "course", you can watch through the video, ...there's also resources listed on the right side that are helpful.

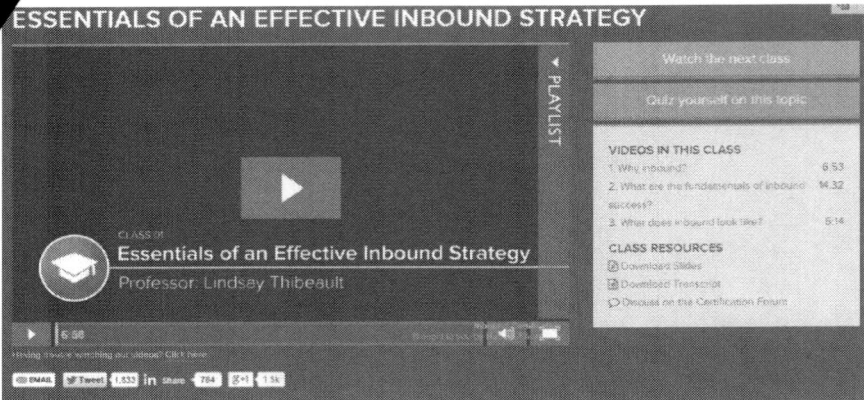

You may also be able to access the course material without an account:
http://academy.hubspot.com/ic15/essentials-of-an-effective-inbound-strategy
> as well as share it on social media, etc.

Starting a Trial

To get a closer look at HubSpot, I'd recommend creating a Trial account. Overall, it's oriented for someone with a website, and one crucial piece that can make it come alive is being able to take a HubSpot code, and add it to your site, so that you can see the full impact. If you want to do that, you "might" want to consider setting up a new Wordpress site, or getting some assistance from a Web developer, to set up a test.

If you're new to all these things, I wouldn't worry about it – the tracking part isn't critical for trying out HubSpot's features, but it's a "nice to have". Remember the idea of accessing Help, writing down the HubSpot phone number when you start your account, so that you have someone to call.

To begin, visit www.hubspot.com and click the Free Trial button at the top.

The website address you enter here can be changed, but it might be worth considering making some kind of test site (or if you already have a company website, either adding the tracking later or getting someone to do it for you.). HubSpot won't hurt your existing website – the code part is to be able to help track the impact of marketing automation.

There's no one way to try things, so I'd just pick a website address you have, either your main one, or a test one (ex: a new test domain name registered at godaddy.com, along with a "managed wordpress site"), and enter it on the first page of the sign-up.

Welcome.

You now have access to all of HubSpot's tools. Next, let's customize those tools to match your needs

Is this your website? ?

www.casamarketing.org

Yes

Step 1 of 6

Continue

Then click Continue.

TIP: Another thing I'd suggest is reading through this entire section, the entire chapter, even, before actually trying anything, as a learning experience – make a few notes, and "then" come back and try a few things out, with support phone numbers ready at hand.

With HubSpot, you'll gather a remarkable amount of data.

We track it all

📑 Page views

📧 Form submissions

✉ Email open rates

★ And so much more

This page is just talking about the kinds of things you can track. Click Continue

Continue

Then, especially if you've ever visited HubSpot before, downloaded one of their ebooks, perhaps, you'll get a taste of personalized marketing automation. You're a "lead" for HubSpot, so then they may display a message directly to you:

Let's use you as an example, Todd.

We've tracked your interactions with the HubSpot website using the same technology you'll be using to track your own leads

Then you might get an additional message:

This is how you appear in the HubSpot database

Which means this is how your contacts appear in your own database.

Todd, we first met   a few seconds ago

How can I track my customers?

And if you like you can click the "How can I" button.

Next, you'll get the "pitch" for installing the tracking code – again, not critically necessary if you're just kicking the tires, but maybe something you'd like to try.

Track everything your visitors do.

All it takes to start is a one-time installation of your HubSpot tracking code.

★ The original source of the customer
(e.g., weorganic, paid, social)

📇 Website visits

🗒 Landing page views

🗐 Form submits

💬 Social media mentions

✉ Emails delivered

✉ Email opens

✔ Email clicks

[Install HubSpot tracking code]

Then you'll want to click the "Install" button at the bottom, to see what's there. It doesn't install anything, it just gives you information on *how* to do it.

Here's where you can click buttons to either do it yourself or send the instructions. I'd suggest emailing the instructions to yourself, even if you don't have a web developer, and if you want to dive in, try making a test wordpress site and asking Godaddy support to help you put in the code (or HubSpot, or both).

Install your HubSpot Tracking Code.

Installs just like Google Analytics.

Option #1: Install myself

Choose this option if you can make changes to your website code

OR

Option #2: Send instructions

Choose this option if you typically have an IT or web developer make changes to your website code

View instructions

Send instructions by email

We'll take a look at the "Install myself" option, so you can see what it might look like.

HubSpot tracking code instructions

✕

Your tracking code

Copy this code and place it before </body> tag on each website page.

```
<!-- Start of Async HubSpot Analytics Code -->
  <script type="text/javascript">
    (function(d,s,i,r) {
      if (d.getElementById(i)){return;}
      var
n=d.createElement(s),e=d.getElementsByTagName(s)[0];
      n.id=i;n.src='//js.hs-analytics.net/analytics
/'+(Math.ceil(new Date()/r)*r)+'/681638.js';
      e.parentNode.insertBefore(n, e);
    })(document,"script","hs-analytics",300000);
  </script>
```

WordPress sites

Use the HubSpot WordPress plugin to install your tracking code.

Your Hub ID is **681638**

Done

So basically you copy and paste this code, put it in the right place in your website, and you're good to go – it helps for tracking the results of marketing automation campaigns. And if you have a Wordpress site, it's a little easier – you can use a "plug-in" and enter your HubSpot ID, and you're ready to go.

Wordpress / HubSpot

So if you haven't tried Wordpress out, the way it works is it makes it easier to make a customized website, without necessarily having to know as much on the technical side. Agencies, designers use Wordpress increasingly as a platform, and there are a lot of "plug-ins", that make it easy to add features to the site, at the click of a button, basically.

So in HubSpot, on the "tracking code" page, when you are filling out an account, you may want to click on the wordpress plug-in link: (and make note of your HubSpot ID)

WordPress sites

Use the HubSpot WordPress plugin to install your tracking code.

Your Hub ID is **681638**

The direct link to the resulting page is available at: https://wordpress.org/plugins/hubspot/installation/

And it basically gives you a simple set of instructions for installing the plug-in. HubSpot support may also be able to help you, or a web hosting company (Ex: if you try making a managed wordpress account at Godaddy and call their support line)

Installing the Plugin

(using the WordPress Admin Console)

1. From your dashboard, click on "Plugins" in the left sidebar
2. Add a new plugin
3. Search for "HubSpot"
4. Install "HubSpot for WordPress"
5. Once Installed, click on the HubSpot plugin in your sidebar and go to "settings"
6. Enter your Hub ID and authorize the plugin to access your HubSpot account (your Hub ID can be found with the product version at the bottom of your HubSpot Dashboard. Once you've entered it into the plugin settings, click the Click here to authenticate button. You'll be asked to login to HubSpot and give access).

In this next section, I'll give you a high-level view of what it looks like, jumping into the Dashboard of a Wordpress website. Basically you select the Plug-ins feature in the navigation, and click Add New:

Plugins Add New

Then there are any number of Wordpress plug-ins you may want to try, but for now, I'd just try the HubSpot plug-in:

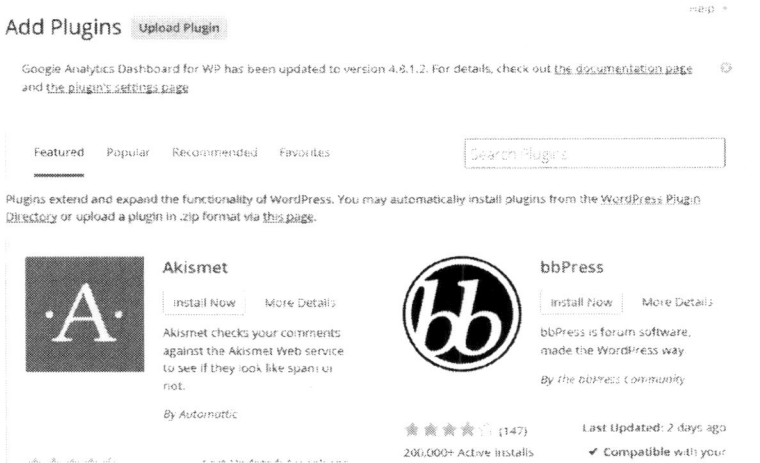

You can click the Search Plugins box, and type in HubSpot, and look for this:

And you can click Install Now.

This is in some ways an example of marketing automation – or at least automation – the wordpress platform is designed to make it easier to add features to a website, saving either you or a Web developer time, hassle and headache.

Once the plugin is installed, then you click Activate Plugin:

Then, it's added to your website, and you can click Settings:

HubSpot for WordPress
Settings Deactivate Edit

The HubSpot for WordPress plugin integrates the power of HubSpot with your WordPress site

Version 1.9.4 | By HubSpot | View details

And this is where it may be easier to try a test site to try out HubSpot, if you don't have a Web developer or just want to try it yourself, as compared with having to manually put the code in the right place on your website. By putting the plugin in Wordpress, you get this far and then all you have to do is click the Enter your HubSpot ID link:

General HubSpot Settings

Almost done! Enter your HubSpot Hub ID and you'll be ready to rock.

And to review, you could get this from the Free Trial signup wizard (it won't be the number below, it will be *your* ID)

WordPress sites

Use the HubSpot WordPress plugin to install your tracking code

Your Hub ID is **681638**

HubSpot Hub ID

681638

Activate HubSpot for WordPress

Then enter it in, and click the Activate button.

I can't tell you that for many people, it's so much easier to do it this way, than the manual way.

(If you're curious about Wordpress, feel free to check out my book on Wordpress on Amazon, under "Todd Kelsey Wordpress".)

Finish Configuring HubSpot

So if you're following along in the wizard, after you hit the Tracking page . . .

Install your HubSpot Tracking Code.

Installs just like Google Analytics

Option #1: Install myself

Choose this option if you can make changes to your website code.

OR

Option #2: Send instructions

Choose this option if you typically have an IT or web developer make changes to your website code.

View instructions

Send instructions by email

Step 5 of 6

Continue

. . . .you can just click the Continue button at the bottom.

If you followed the steps you might see a screen like this:

Nice Work.

You've customized your HubSpot account with a few personal details. Now let's go have some fun

Whool Let's get HubSpotting

Get Started

And then you can click the Get started button.

If you end up back in HubSpot without this "wizard", you can always go back to it through the Getting Started button at the top right of the HubSpot screen when you're logged in.

Getting Started With HubSpot

So some readers may want to follow this wizard; we aren't going to follow everything, but we'll take a look at Landing Pages.

Getting started
Ready to start making a splash with HubSpot? Here are a few easy first steps to get you started

Profile progress ●

○ Add HubSpot to your website and marketing channels
The core action that drives all of HubSpot. Installing the HubSpot tracking code allows you to track all visitor activity over all your marketing channels.

○ Embed a HubSpot form on your website to generate leads
Replace or create a form on your website to start automatically gathering leads in your HubSpot database. We'll create a list of these leads automatically.

○ Choose a theme for your pages
Your theme will be fully responsive and beautiful out of the box. Pick your favorite one of 5 themes to spruce up your Landing Pages, Blog, and Site Pages.

○ Create your first landing page
Select a responsive template or create your own. Enter your content in the WYSIWYG editor.

Creating a Landing Page

If you like try clicking on the create your first landing page link:

○ Create your first landing page
Select a responsive template or create your own. Enter your content in the WYSIWYG editor.

There's two ways to go – you "might" get a sample landing page in your account, which you can explore. A landing page is the place, or tool that you use to "attract" your inbound leads – understanding the principles is one of the things that will make the nuts and bolts of this make more sense – that's why I recommend going through the HubSpot training mentioned earlier.

Landing Pages

HubSpot has a sample page that may go in your account, which you can try and customize as you like:

Title:

Sample - Convert visitors with a HubSpot landing page

Published:
9:52am

Making Your Own Landing Page

If you don't have the sample page, or if you just want to try making one any way, this section reviews the "manual method"

First, click Create a new page:

Create a new page

Then, select a template, like "2 Column Form Right":

Landing Pages » Create a New Landing Page

Template:	
All Templates	15
My Favorites	0
Purchased	0
Hidden	0
Most Used Templates	
Recently Used Templates	

All folders

No preview available

2 Column Form Right

HubSpot Templates:

Example Templates   23

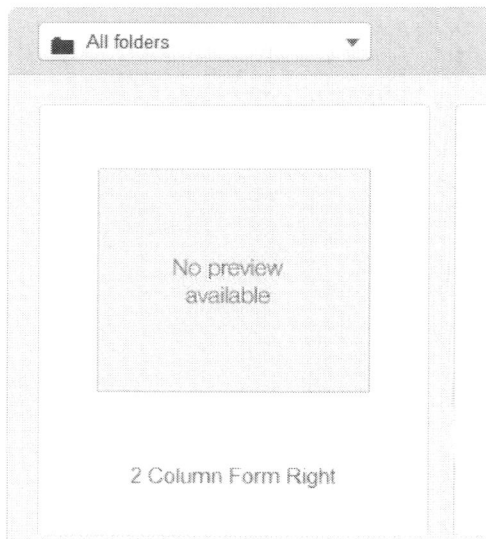

Just click on it to select it:

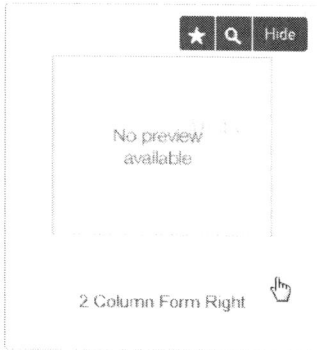

Then enter a page name like "My Landing Page":

And whatever you do in HubSpot, be on the lookout for tutorials you can click on:

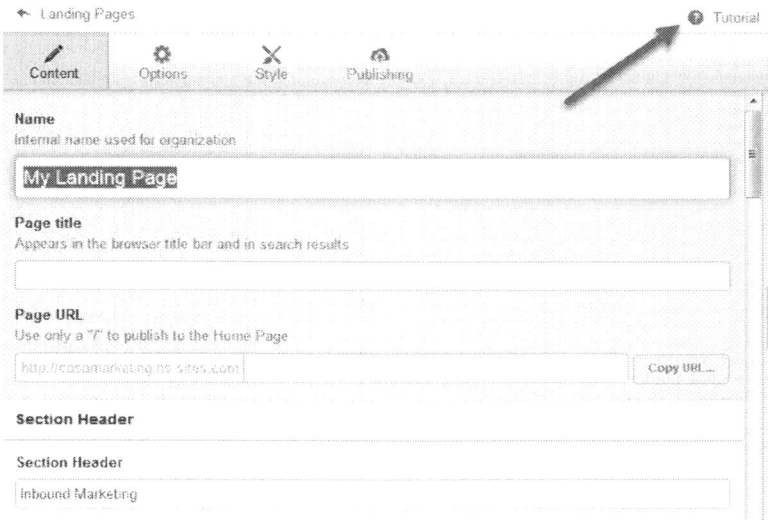

Next, you can create a page title – the title doesn't matter too much for testing:

Name
Internal name used for organization

My Landing Page

Page title
Appears in the browser title bar and in search results

Social Media Marketing Book

Page URL
Use only a "/" to publish to the Home Page

http://casamarketing.hs-sites.com | social-media-marketing-book | Copy URL...

And you'll see that there's a "COPY URL" button – this will end up being the link where you can try the landing page. The scenario is, you have a landing page out there, that you share by social media, or an ad campaign, or it's just sitting out there listed on search engines. It has some kind of compelling offer (tip: take the HubSpot training!), and people are "landing" on this page. The goal is to get them to enter their contact information so you can follow up.

Here's the sample URL I made, which may still be active when you read this:
http://casamarketing.hs-sites.com/social-media-marketing-book

Next, I'd just suggest scrolling down through the various options and checking things out. You can adjust things if you like, change settings, but for now, you may just want to keep it simple.

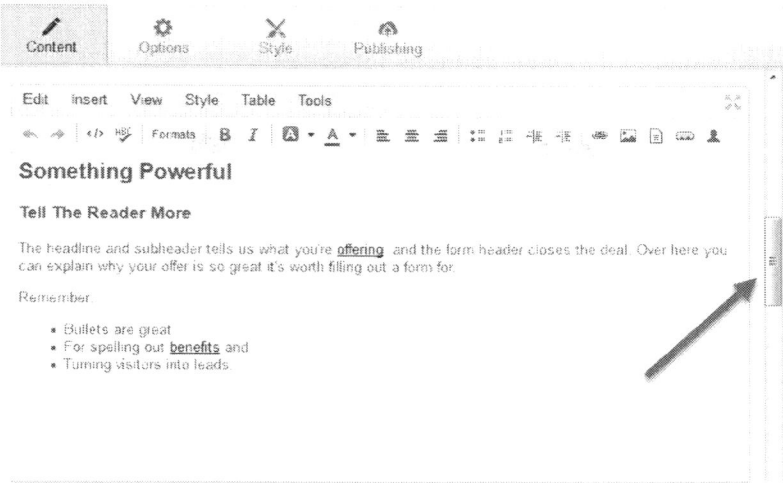

The part where you definitely have to enter something in is the Form. Try clicking on the Select a Form menu and choosing the Default Form:

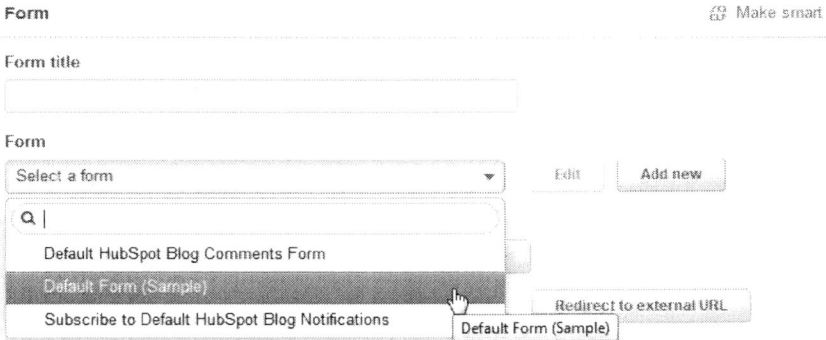

Then directly below, click the Display an inline thank you message:

And finally, click the Publish button:

| Publish | Save | Actions ▼ |

Ready? Click Publish page now:

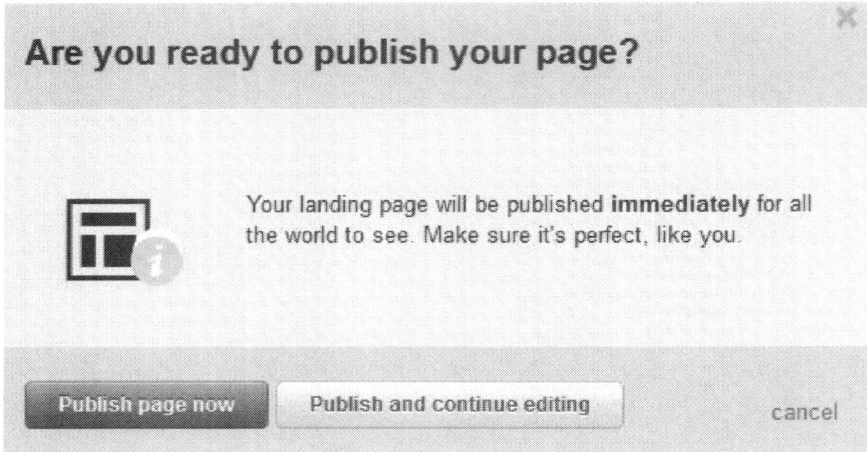

Are you ready to publish your page? ✕

Your landing page will be published **immediately** for all the world to see. Make sure it's perfect, like you.

| Publish page now | Publish and continue editing | cancel |

Then, in theory, you'll have a preview that looks something like this:

Back to: Landing Pages

● My Landing Page 🖉

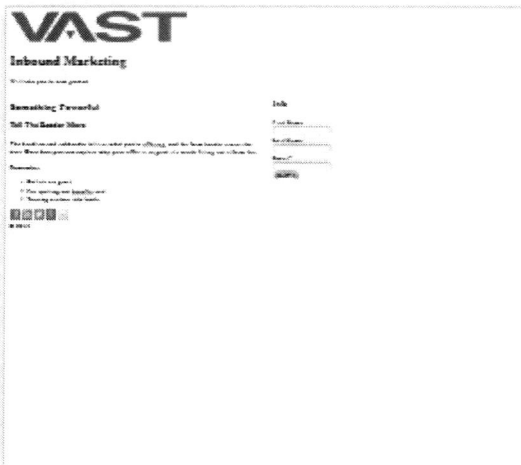

And if you need to, in the navigation, you can scroll down and get the "public link" to try it out:

Landing Page Actions

View Live

Unpublish

Edit

Clone

View Revisions

Archive

Delete

Public link

http://casamarketing.hs-sites.com/social-m

And in this case, if my link is still active, you can try it out here:

http://casamarketing.hs-sites.com/social-media-marketing-book

Depending on what you did, your sample page will look something like this:

VAST

Inbound Marketing

Will take you to new ground

Something Powerful

Tell The Reader More

The headline and subheader tells us what you're offering, and the form header closes the deal. Over here you can explain why your offer is so great it's worth filling out a form for.

Remember:

- Bullets are great
- For spelling out benefits and
- Turning visitors into leads.

Info

First Name

Last Name

Email*

Submit

© 2015

So, try filling out the form!

Info

First Name

John

Last Name

Tester

Email*

d.e.kelsey@gmail.com

Submit

Using the Example Landing Page

If you do have a sample page and want to try it, click on the gear icon on the right, and select Edit:

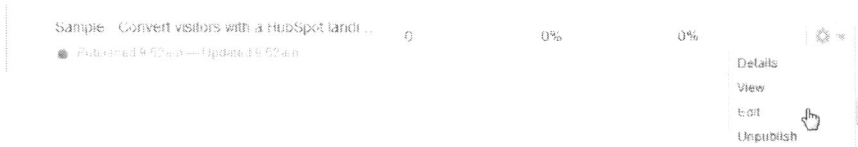

Then literally without needing to make any changes, you can scroll down and click the Copy URL button:

And then try out the sample form – here's "my" link, which may still be active:
http://casamarketing.hs-sites.com/offer

VAST

Welcome to your HubTheme Landing Page

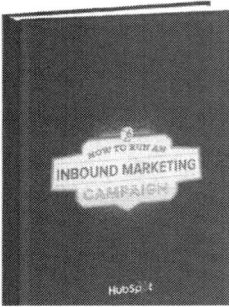

A great landing page conveys the value that a visitor will receive in exchange for filling out your form. What's in it for them?

Your landing page should be:

- Short
- Concise
- Clean

Bullets work great. So does header text.

In HubSpot, the Landing Pages tool is closely linked with the Forms and Call-to-Action tools. Create a call-to-action to

First Name

John

Last Name

Tester

Email*

todd.e.kelsey@gmail.com

Submit

It will look a bit more polished. So, try filling out the form!

HubSpot Dashboard

Next, in our whirlwind ride through HubSpot, try going back to the Dashboard (after you've set up a landing page and tried out the form)

Marketing   Dashboard

In theory, you should see some leads coming in. Exciting! This is where the magic happens. You connect your site, make a landing page, create a campaign, put all the pieces together, and attempt to attract leads. This chapter isn't trying to be comprehensive about HubSpot – just a high-level introduction. To learn all the related strategy, I highly recommend going through HubSpot Inbound Marketing Certification courses first, and maybe checking out some of their other resources.

Contacts All Time   Add Persona

Total	Leads	Marketing Qualified Contacts	Customers
3	3	0	0

Segment your contacts for better targeting — Add Persona

So now that you've got some Contacts, let's check them out!

You can go to the top of the screen in HubSpot, select Contacts, and Contacts Home:

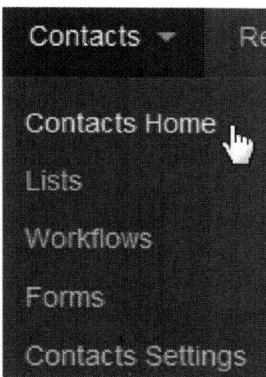

Contacts ▾   Re

Contacts Home

Lists

Workflows

Forms

Contacts Settings

And then you should see real live contacts, who you've attracted to become Leads (ok, it's you testing the form, but it's representative, right?)

Add to lists   Enroll in workflow   Delete

Name	Created On
Todd Kelsey	Jul 15 2015 1:37 PM
John Tester 2	Jul 15 2015 1:20 PM

HubSpot Workflows

HubSpot Workflows can be as customized and as complicated as you like. If you haven't read the Mailchimp automation chapter, you may want to start there. Also HubSpot has a lot of good training material. But like Infusionsoft, and other marketing automation systems, the "workflow" is where a lot of the magic happens, as you plan out how to "nurture leads".

To access workflows, select Contacts > Workflows:

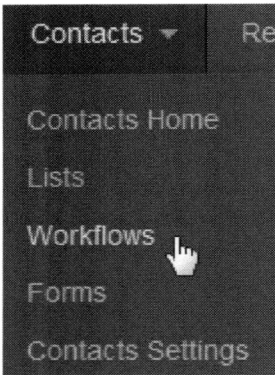

And be sure to explore the Tutorial links. You can create a workflow manually, but HubSpot also has "recipes", which is their version of a campaign template, which can be customized, and are a great way to learn.

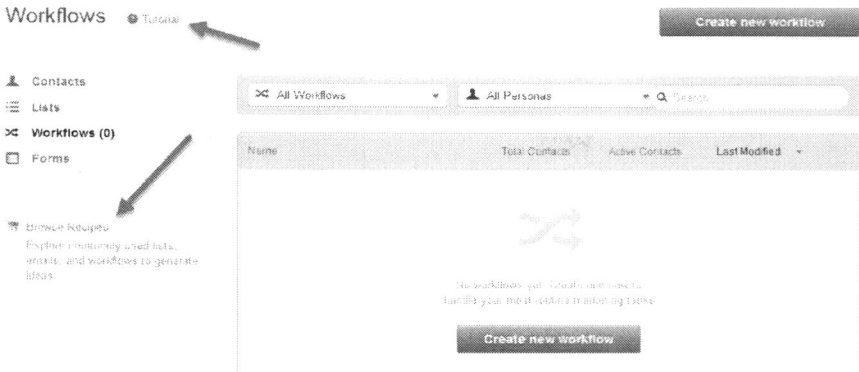

So try clicking on the Browse Recipes link, and the first thing we'll need to do is make sure we're compliant with CAN-SPAM.

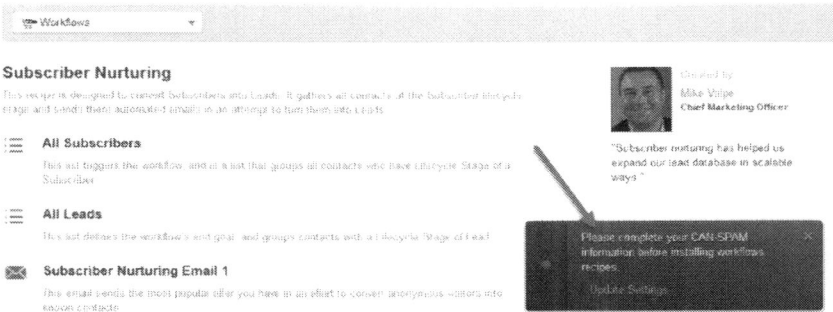

So click on Update Settings:

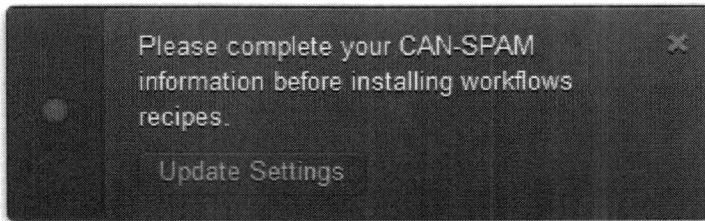

And then enter in basic information – this is to make sure you follow best practices of sending out emails – you can enter as little as the company name and physical address:

Email Footer Information

Company Name *	CASA Marketing
Address *	P.O. Box 1302
Address Line 2	
City *	Wheaton
State *	IL
Zip Code	
Country	
Phone Number	

Required for all email sent from HubSpot.

Save changes

Next, you'll need to get back to Workflows:

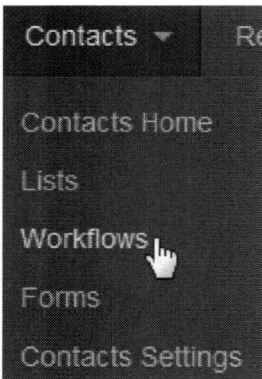

Contacts ▼   Re

Contacts Home

Lists

Workflows

Forms

Contacts Settings

And Browse Recipes:

🛒 Browse Recipes
Explore commonly used lists,
emails, and workflows to generate
ideas.

Then you'll see something like this:

Subscriber Nurturing

This recipe is designed to convert Subscribers into Leads. It gathers all contacts at the Subscriber lifecycle stage and sends them automated emails in an attempt to turn them into Leads.

☰ All Subscribers

This list triggers the workflow, and is a list that groups all contacts who have Lifecycle Stage of a Subscriber.

☰ All Leads

This list defines the workflow's end goal, and groups contacts with a Lifecycle Stage of Lead.

✉ Subscriber Nurturing Email 1

This email sends the most popular offer you have in an effort to convert anonymous visitors into known contacts.

✉ Subscriber Nurturing Email 2

This email sends a second offer that has also proven effective for you in the past.

⤭ Subscriber Workflows

This workflow ties it all together, sending two emails in succession to the starting list of contacts to turn them into Leads.

And you can click Add this recipe:

Add this recipe

It will take a moment or two to install:

Your recipe is cooking   ✕

The **Subscriber Nurturing** recipe could take a few seconds to cook. We'll link you to it once it cooks, but if you'd like to explore, it'll be on the workflows page.

Then you can click View Workflow:

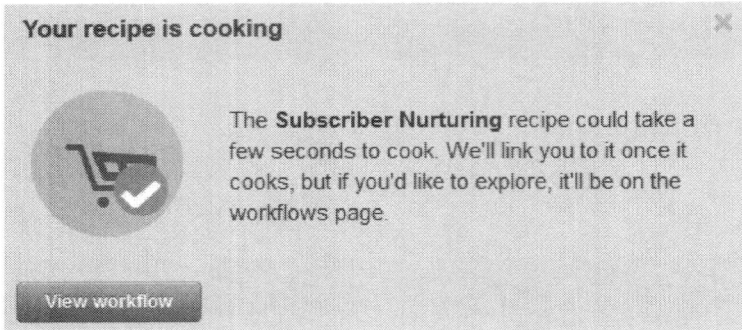

Your recipe is cooking   ✕

The **Subscriber Nurturing** recipe could take a few seconds to cook. We'll link you to it once it cooks, but if you'd like to explore, it'll be on the workflows page.

View workflow

The next thing you'll run into is a possible message that you might need to ask for Workflows to be enabled:

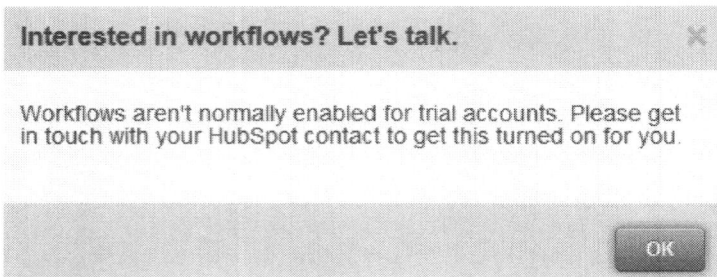

Interested in workflows? Let's talk.   ✕

Workflows aren't normally enabled for trial accounts. Please get in touch with your HubSpot contact to get this turned on for you.

OK

Nevertheless, you can still see what's "in" the workflow, and you'll see some of the way HubSpot suggests starting out a nurture sequence:

You send emails out, wait, send more:

It's part art, part science – and that's why going through the training will help, as well as talking to customers, trying out things, getting their feedback, tweaking marketing automation in a way that's right for *your* business.

Congratulations on making it through the hands-on portion of the chapter. Now on to some Industry Perspective!

Industry Perspective: My HubSpot Experience

Jim Cooper
Marketing Automation Expert

Todd: Did you have an aha moment when you were learning about HubSpot, in terms of seeing its potential? If so, when did you realize what it could do?

Jim: Learning the so-called "Inbound Methodology" has been hugely helpful. If I had to identify an "aha" moment, it was within the first few online courses I sat through where HubSpot outlined their rendition of the marketing funnel: **Awareness > Consideration > Decision.** Really simple, but a much better way to think about and map micro- and macro-conversions than **Top > Middle > Bottom.** I found it / find it to be really enlightening, and when explaining it to clients - some of whom have logged decades in marketing management - they are similarly impressed.

After trying various inbound marketing campaigns, are there any high-level strategies that you found most effective?

The first step in any inbound marketing campaign is assessing KPI's in analytics data and ensuring the stats are tracking correctly, whether in Google Analytics, HubSpot, Salesforce... whatever. Any app integrations have to be clean, and they must play nicely with one another. Each piece of content, each Call To Action, each engagement opportunity must to be attached to an analytics number - otherwise there is no way to keep score.

Additionally, HubSpot's "buyer persona" propaganda is right on the money (literally and figuratively). Personas developed through proper research are the keys to any effective inbound campaign - without them, any content produced / keyword research executed /

stats analyzed is just "sound and fury, signifying nothing." Whom are you targeting and why? Who brings your firm the most revenue and why? Where do they go for their info? What are they talking about, and what are their pain points? Those are the questions to ask.

When learning HubSpot, what was the most interesting thing to you that stuck out? What do you most appreciate about he platform?

HubSpot Inbound Methodology. Boom. It's tightly organized and, as I'm discovering in my client work, really effective - regardless of what apps you're using (HubSpot included). I have the Inbound Methodology permanently pinned to a corkboard that is within my sight line for reference every workday, so I never lose sight of the big picture. Specific to HubSpot, the way the software handles contacts, lists and workflows is really powerful. Additionally, the stats engine - when used in combination with Google Analytics - really cuts down on statistical noise so you can accurately assess content / website performance. Also really useful to track behavior funnels and to see how people engage with content in real-time.

What's your least favorite thing - room for improvement, advice for the company?

It would be hugely beneficial for them to tie up any loose ends with respect to their own CRM – which in my experience is a work in progress and has a lot of problems. Once HubSpot's CRM is on par with Salesforce's - a one-stop shop for marketers AND salespeople - there will be no stopping it.

If you were talking to a small business owner, and they asked about HubSpot, how would you describe the value proposition?

One-stop shop to manage your digital marketing efforts, including email, social media and blogging campaigns. Don't have to use 15 tools - can just use one.

Have you witnessed how HubSpot can help increase revenue and profit that would otherwise be sitting at the table?

Yes. From what I've seen, the tracking features, robust email campaign engine, and list segmenting tools have led to conversions across the board as we've adjusted content strategies based on analytics data.

Ever tried other marketing automation platforms - any idea of how they compare?

Working with a client who's on Pardot now, and sat through Pardot's sales presentation last year. My client's going to give me a quick demo of their application of Pardot next week. As of yet, haven't seen anything else. Pardot seems to work similarly to HubSpot, but with native Salesforce integration, as it's a Salesforce product.

What's your opinion on leveraging social alongside HubSpot? Depends on the business? Or focus on the main platform?

Depends on the business, in terms of dredging viable qualified leads from social. But regardless of industry, HubSpot's social monitoring tool can help a lot with keyword research.

What strategies have you used to develop content for inbound marketing? Partnership between in-house experts and outsourcing? Did you ever try writing all the material yourself? Any perspective on doing it all in-house vs outsourcing content?

Again, depends on the business/industry. No one person can write it all, and a common problem across many clients has been finding (a) dependable content writer(s) / creator(s). "Engaging content" doesn't cut it any more, either - it has to be what Rand Fishkin at Moz calls "10x content" - meaning the best content in the industry that is scalable.

Do you think the market is saturated or that you can have a competitive edge by trying marketing automation?

I don't think the market is saturated at all - in fact, most companies aren't even considering SEO when launched their corporate sites, from what I'm seeing. It's amazing, but over and over again I see companies missing gigantic opportunities.

If more people are using marketing automation, how do you stand out with your content to attract customers? Quality?

Again, the content has to not only optimized, engaging and relevant - it has to be the best. Why should I spend an extra second reading your blog when your competitor's is better? I suppose the "how" is research - what are your competitors or thought leaders in your industry doing to maximize engagements? What are people talking about? Why is a particular piece more popular than another?

Conclusion/Discussion

Congratulations on making it through the HubSpot chapter, and getting some hands-on experience!

This rounds out the general tour of marketing automation. In the next chapter, we'll take a look at the theme of "going beyond pay per click advertising", with industry perspective from Bill Crawford.

If you're ready to take things to the next level, you're also welcome to schedule a free consultation, to see how Rainmaker Internet Marketing can help your business make use of marketing automation. Please visit rainma.com/automation

Learning More

Here's some links to get you started.

HubSpot ranked #1 in G2Crowd's Marketing Automation Report 2014
https://www.g2crowd.com/categories/marketing-automation

HubSpot ranked #1 in VentureBeat's Marketing Automation Index 2014
http://venturebeat.com/2014/02/26/top-10-marketing-automation-companies-the-vb-index-report/

Summer 2015 Grid℠ Report: Marketing Automation Software Rankings
http://about.g2crowd.com/blog/best-marketing-automation-software-summer-2015/
> Timely Summer 2015 article, HubSpot tops ratings, Infusionsoft comes in top 6, mentions some other platforms

http://offers.hubspot.com/free-ebook-an-introduction-to-lead-nurturing
> In this free ebook, you'll learn:
> The specific benefits of lead nurturing
> How to set up a lead nurturing campaign
> What types of lead nurturing campaigns you can create
> How to optimize your lead nurturing emails

30 Thought-Provoking Lead Nurturing Stats You Can't Ignore
http://blog.hubspot.com/blog/tabid/6307/bid/30901/30-Thought-Provoking-Lead-Nurturing-Stats-You-Can-t-Ignore.aspx

How Marketing Can Work With Sales to Close More (and Better) Leads
http://blog.hubspot.com/marketing/marketing-sales-close-leads

For More Information

For a complete list of links and resources, visit rainma.com/book

Chapter 10: Going Beyond Google Ads

Bill Crawford,
Founder and President of
Rainmaker Internet Marketing

Introduction

In this chapter, to help round things out in a conversational style, getting some insight from Bill Crawford, on several topics related to marketing automation.

When you're reading this book, if you're ready to take things to the next level, you're also welcome to schedule a free consultation, to see how Rainmaker Internet Marketing can help your business make use of marketing automation. Please visit rainma.com/automation

A Plumber That's Crushing It

An example of a local service provider Bill noticed, who is doing it right.

Todd: So you came across an example of a plumber who is crushing it with their marketing strategy. How did you come across them?

Bill: I did a search for plumber. I looked for the one with the most customer reviews. And they happened to be local.

What got your attention about their campaign? Anything stick out to you?

When I received the email the day before the appointment, called "Meet the Team", with a picture of a guy coming to my house the next day, I knew this company had their act together. The personal detail made the difference.

What's the complete set, with the various pieces of the strategy?

1) First there was a meet the team email.
2) Then the guy showed up. At the end of the job he presented a card and asked for a review. I was impressed with the card.

3) Later that evening I got a follow up requesting a review.

On the card itself, on one side it said something like: "Want to give a review to your service provider?" and also invited feedback. And on the card there were simple steps, saying where to go, asking the person to write a review. On the other side of the card, the steps were repeated, with the address for the website, the name of the service provider, and the company name. And verbiage like "It only takes a minute". So it was a simple thing, but reviews are huge, so it's a good thing to leave a simple physical reminder in someone's hand.

They had the emails in place, and card. A great example of end to end marketing and customer follow-up.

Another thing I was impressed with - in 2 days, I hadn't yet taken action, and I got an email "I noticed you haven't given us any feedback yet - we'd love to get your feedback."

So it wasn't making any assumptions - it was actively soliciting feedback (and hoping for the best).

What's the role of customer reviews in their system?

This contractor understands the importance of customer reviews. For local search, it's really important to have good reviews on your Google + page, because when people are out there searching, the reviews are a strong impact on their choice to call a particular service provider. It's just like reviews on Amazon about books.

So how does marketing automation fit in?

So these emails that I received were put in motion by a system in the background. A lot of connection happened with me, through their email. Inside the company, it took very little effort. It was the right sequence of emails, in the right timing. The welcome email saying someone was coming out, with their picture. Then, asking nicely if I could give feedback a couple days later.

What are the lessons for other local service providers? What should they keep in mind?

From a lead generation perspective, customer reviews are absolutely critical. You need to keep a light touch in asking for them, and it's good to frame it by asking for feedback, in case someone had a negative experience. But ideally you are out there putting quality into the job, and making it as simple as possible to give that review.

Every company should have an automated way to make it easy for people to give reviews and get them in the right places. It's not just a system, it's a culture, and it's ongoing.

In the era of where the customer is in charge, and anyone can air dirty laundry on social media, a company wants an unhappy customer to come to them first - before they go to one of the endless number of consumer advocate sites or social media outlets. So it's about maintaining an open feedback loop with the customer.

At what point can an agency step in and help with things like this?

An agency that does marketing automation can help set campaigns in motion, and help optimize them as you find out the right message for your customers. An agency can help with the heavy lifting, so you can focus on your business and the customer conversation.

Also, an experienced agency knows the right questions to ask, in order to help put together the right message.

In the next chapter, there's a great case study about Brian Young at Home Painters of Toronto. It's no secret that his success also came at a cost - it requires time. And he's also straight up about the investment of resources. So the reality is that to achieve that level of amazing success in terms of increasing his revenue, staff, competitiveness - he was mentored by business coaches and consultants. In this industry, 90% of the people don't reach that level of success. And part of the reason is understandable - there's the challenges to deal with. But an agency can come alongside and help you with those challenges, so it's not all on you.

For example, a sustained effort to increase your revenues by a million a year might be doable, but part of that investment might be spending a reasonable amount for the assistance.

For example, I won't even sell an Infusionsoft app unless the situation is a good fit and they are ready for the software. There's teamwork between an agency and the client. And I think Brian's case study is a case in point, where he talks about the fact that when you're implementing marketing automation, it's not just making a new system, it's actually taking a closer look at your own business, and that's part of the real value; it forces you to analyze your business, the way you do business. And that's worth investing in.

In spite of the challenges, I think it's important to point out that people can get success in using the software at the beginning. You don't have to wait years to see an impact. So generally what happens is that you can succeed right away, such as setting the target of implementing an email blast with 100 customers.

So even if you just get 100 customer emails into a system, send an email out, and get 20 opt-ins, that kind of milestone gets you going. In Brian's interview you'll see that he did things incrementally. He discovered initially that just getting his customer emails in a system helped him get off to a good start.

PPC with No Follow-Up: A Gap to Fill

Why marketing automation is so important for the bottom line. If a company has no marketing automation they're leaving money at the table.

Todd: So is your view that a company without marketing automation is leaving money at the table?

Bill: Yes. We call this throwing money in the garbage. You have to advertise one way or another to get people to visit your Website, but the industry average is that 97% of the people who go to a website don't opt-in to anything. So if there's a way to *reduce* that substantially, it's a way to make your money work more efficiently.

So how does lead capture relate?

So when they visit, a prospect may not be ready to call yet. But every business has something that could be used to help nurture that prospect. That's the basic idea of inbound marketing. Examples of common lead capture techniques are: ebook downloads, a checklist, tip sheets, free kits -- something that offers the customer enough value for giving contact information. That captures the lead and gives you a basis for following up and seeing if they'd like more information, a consultation, or to set up a free inspection, etc.

What about companies who are generating revenue, doing just fine with standard digital marketing? Why they do need to go beyond pay per click?

It's a fast paced industry - as things get more competitive, as efficiency improves, the stakes get higher. So in order to get the best return on advertising spend, you need to keep up with the times.

Would you say that marketing automation is also about a balance between outbound marketing (ex: pay per click) and inbound marketing?

Yes, when the two are put together, they can work very efficiently. You have a message going out, but you also are doing your best to capture leads and lose them as little as possible when you do get them to your site. It complements a good website design that's optimized for the best customer experience, including content to attract customers (the inbound marketing mentality)

From what you've seen, can you rely consistently "only" on pay per click, or do you need to supplement it with inbound marketing?

Yesterday I spoke with a customer who spends 12k/month on pay per click. They have no SEO or marketing automation. So with SEO and marketing automation, the value proposition is that they can spend less, to get more leads, because they are doing things more efficiently, and capturing more customers. Nurturing leads, not allowing good prospects to fall through the cracks or be captured elsewhere. There's better follow up.

From a competitive standpoint, what kind of edge does marketing automation give you?

For our industry, for example, in marketing services, we know there's over 5,000 Google partners worldwide who offer pay per click management services. And a very small percentage of those offer marketing automation as well. When you put these two together, we can offer a better ROI for advertising spend. So the combination sets us apart, and helps us set our clients apart.

Is there any way to ease into marketing automation? What's the first step if you're doing PPC and want to increase your efficiency with automation?

You can ease into Marketing Automation. My recommendation is, don't get into it until you are serious about implementing it into your company. Life is too busy to just dabble in marketing automation. My concern is, unless it is a priority, it will get pushed to the side and you will not take advantage of it.

If you are doing PPC and want to get a better return for your money with marketing automation, the first place to start is the landing page from the PPC campaigns. I would want you to ask the following questions: What is the offer to the prospect? Why this? Have you tried other offers? What kind of follow up sequence is there? Short term nurture? Long Term Nurture? What kind of results are you getting now? etc.

Over the years, you've seen the rise of different forms of digital marketing - when did you first encounter marketing automation, and consider going beyond PPC? What convinced you?

6 years ago I saw Perry Marshall, a marketing industry expert, using Infusionsoft. I was impressed, and dove in to start learning about the product. What impressed me the most was for me to receive a personalized email, as a follow up. It was specifically based on a previous response, something I indicated interested in. The email was not generic. That's where Infusionsoft sets themselves apart - with that level of targeted follow up.

Lifecycle Marketing

In order to form the best strategy, you need to base it on looking at the full life cycle of your customers. There's a lot of low-hanging fruit out there, with lead capture/nurture, upselling customers, and making sure to get feedback, then showing the results with reviews..

Todd: What is lifecycle marketing?

Bill: Life cycle marketing is a way to map the customer journey from the initial stages of being a prospect all the way through the purchase level, additional purchases, and receiving referrals as well.

How do you figure out what the lifecycle is for your clients?

Usually new clients are not aware of it and haven't thought in those terms before, so it's a learning experience. I ask them how they get their customers, what their lead sources are, what their sales process is, whether it's a one-time sale or additional sale.

We'll also ask questions like:
- What it your the Customer Lifetime Value?
  (If they know it. CLV = during the relationship with that customer, what dollar amount of revenue does that customer bring in.)
- How long do customers stay with you?
- What is the total profit per customer?
- What is your sales process?

So with lifecycle marketing, lead capturing is the first step? What's the best way to capture leads on the Internet?

It really depends on the business. Generally speaking, you want to offer valuable content to the prospect that they would want to learn about, which is a stepping stone towards a purchase. For example, you could offer an ebook or cheat sheet, checklist, some kind of resource. It has to have enough value and worth for a customer to be willing to give up their email for.

Once you've captured leads into being customers, how do you upsell them?

What's most important before thinking about upselling is to wow them - to what Dan Kennedy refers to as "shock and awe". Seth Gonin calls it the "Purple Cow". You need to overdeliver on what they're expecting, so that they're amazed at your services, so that they want to tell their family and friends about it. Your product or service has to say what you promised it would do. This gives you a foundation to approach them with the option of additional services and products. It's really important early on in the sales process, that they become aware that you offer these additional services and products.

Early on, there was a time we were providing pay per click services to a customer in Florida, and after a year of providing pay per click, they called us to say that they had hired a search engine optimization company. I asked if they had considered hiring us to do that work, and they said "we didn't know that you offered that service". That was a valuable learn. It's so important early on that they're educated about all of your services.

So now, with every new client we have a welcome sequence, and on the second day, we inform them of all our other services. This complements the conversation that happens in the initial sales call as well.

Is another low-hanging fruit referrals or reviews? Is that driven by keeping customers happy?

They key to reviews and referrals is over-delivering, but also making sure to ask for reviews and referrals at the right time. You have to ask the question. When would a client be most willing to provide a review or referral? The answer is when they're happiest.

So when is a client most happiest? It's just about right when you're giving them the best result. It varies by industry. In a home improvement service, it's usually right after they've completed the work.

Is the downside of not having a system in place, which leads fall through the cracks? Have you experienced that yourself?

Sales reps tend to follow up with the deals they can close. If only 25% of deals get closed in the initial interactions, there's a significant amount of potential deals that are sitting at the table, which may take longer to nurture, and marketing automation can help you close some of those deals, which a sales force may otherwise overlook. With marketing automation, you can stay in front of the prospect, and with lead scoring you can identify when they are moving towards a purchase.

As marketing automation helps you stay in front of the prospect with good quality content in a long-term nurture sequence, you can be notified when your content is being clicked on. This allows you to "score" your leads, and put them in different segments. Some people are looking at the content, others are not. But the group of people in your long term nurture sequence that are looking at the content may get a higher lead score. So this allows you to patiently provide value to the customer in a long-term way, and the ones who are engaged with the material are more likely to respond to some kind of follow up offer.

A notification from a system can happen via email, or their "lead score" can automatically increase, or a product like TurboDial can put a red bar across your screen when someone accesses content, so that you can immediately follow up. (See www.turbodial.biz)

So in today's world, people buy when they're ready to buy. Unless you have a system in place that stays in front of that prospect, then yes, most likely you are leaving business at the table.

Is it true that to retain existing customers is less expensive than acquiring new ones? How does marketing automation help?

Yes, it's almost always cheaper to upsell an existing customer than to acquire a new one. The reason being is that the trust you establish with the existing customer is already in place. They know who you are.

Marketing automation allows you to work with the foundation of that trust, and offer additional products and services.

So does that mean that retaining/upselling is just as important as getting customers in the first place?

I would argue that retaining and upselling are *more* important. That is, make sure you have a good system in place for retaining customers, and don't spend all your effort just on trying to acquire new customers. Perry Marshall does a great job in his book 80/20 – explaining how 80% of your revenue comes from 20% of your customers. So you need to pay special attention to your best customers. CRM/marketing automation allows you to identify who your customers are, what their buying habits are, and this better positions you to know when to offer additional services, and to whom to offer them.

Any tips on techniques for retaining/upselling customers that's you've seen be effective?

Make sure on the initial sales call that the prospect is informed of all of your services. Then, after a specific service, it's important they they're reminded of your additional services. Then as the customer relationship grows, they'll be more likely to come back to you. It's important to revisit your offer for additional products/services at a frequency that makes the most sense for the industry and the relationship.

For retaining, I highly recommend the NetPromoter score. It's a survey, a product, and it allows you to pose that important question, "How likely are you to refer us to family or friends, on a scale of 1-10?" This is really powerful, low-hanging fruit for marketing automation. If they click 9-10 you know they're a fan, 7-8 you may have "missed it" somewhere. 0-6, you've got a problem in your hands.

We send it out once a quarter, with marketing automation. The clients gets three surveys, a 5 second survey, if they don't fill it out. Then we get a task automatically assigned to the account manager, to call the client, to ask them to fill it out. If they click 9-10, they're automatically asked for a referral. If they click 7-8, they'll get an email that says, "Sounds like we've met your expectations, but that there's something else we could do for you - please let us know what that is." If it's 0-6, the manager of the account gets a task automatically assigned and an email notification informing them that they need to call this client and find out what's going on.

What's important is, me as an owner, I get informed that there's an issue as well, and this helps me better manage my company. This helps prevents cancellations.

So marketing automation can help you establish this kind of powerful feedback loop, to help you make sure you are doing everything possible to keep customers happy and retain them.

Industry Perspective: Managing Adwords

Jon Nagle
Account Manager, Pay Per Click Specialist
Rainmaker Internet Marketing

Todd: Where do you start with clients? Keyword research?

Jon: After initial high-level background discussion, we typically start with keyword research using multiple keyword tools. At the same time, we need to find out what is considered a lead or conversion for them and make sure we can achieve that for the client.

How do you pick the right keywords for Google Ads?

With the help of multiple keyword tools such as Google's, we can find what keywords are searched the most. Additionally, we ask the client what their product or service is and ask them how they would find themselves if they were to do a Google search.

How do you tell what popular keywords are?

Google's Keyword Tool shows you how many monthly searches there are on that keyword nationwide, and then you dial that number back for local service providers. The other keyword tools we use also show the monthly search volume. Popular keywords are also decided on by using their competitors as a reference, and seeing which keywords they are using by doing Google searches and by putting them through other tools we use.

What do you think the main advantage of pay per click advertising is?

The biggest advantage to pay per click advertising is that it can have instant results, unlike SEO, where it could take months to take affect. And with a good account structure, you can turn it up and spend more or dial back and spend less day to day.

Was pay per click hard to learn? What was the hardest thing to learn?

Pay per click was very hard and intense to learn at the same time. Coming from not knowing anything about PPC, I had to learn on the fly and had a huge learning curve ahead of me. After several months of daily training videos, phone calls, books read, and just hands on experience within the platform, I was able to learn and implement at the same time. I don't think there is one specific thing that was hard to learn, but the learning never ends because Google changes algorithms or policies all the time, so you have to stay in tune with their changes at all times.

Any general tips for making sure you're maximizing your ad budget?
The biggest tip I could give to anyone would be to always try new things, and keep changing until you find a campaign that works. Then try to beat that campaign with a better one.

Do people often start with a limited budget, and then develop confidence, when they see what it can do?

Yes, most people who are just starting out with PPC say they don't want to spend more than 'X' amount of dollars during a month, and within a month or two, they see their account being "limited by budget", while seeing conversions or leads, and that is when they typically tell us, "Don't cap my budget".

What about Bing? How does it compare to Google Ads?

Honestly, my initial thought about Bing was that it was a joke. When Microsoft AdCenter first came out, it was so dumbed down that anybody could've set up an account. However, now after years of changing and trying to catch up to Google, Bing Ads (formally Microsoft AdCenter) is a million times better than it was and allows you to link your Google account directly to your Bing Ads account and just transfer your campaigns right over. I don't think it is fair to ask of a comparison because there really is no comparison, Bing is a little player in Google's world. Additionally, I think Bing does work better on some levels for different industries, in different locations within the US than Google does.

How do you make sure you're getting the maximum ROI from Google ads?

To maximize ROI, we need to make sure the client is getting leads and sales from the Google AdWords account, by having strategic conversations about how much money they want to spend and how many leads they need to maintain their advertising goals. From there we need to split test ads, keywords, keyword budgets, campaign budgets on a daily to weekly basis and keep moving things around until the both of us are satisfied with the results. Once we get those results, then we try to optimize more at a higher level.

Conclusion/Discussion

Congratulations on making it through the chapter, and getting some industry perspective!

If you're ready to take things to the next level, you're also welcome to schedule a free consultation, to see how Rainmaker Internet Marketing can help your business make use of marketing automation. Please visit rainma.com/automation

For More Information

For a complete list of links and resources, visit rainma.com/book

Chapter 11: Case Study – Brian Young of Home Painters Toronto

NOTE FROM THE AUTHOR: Of all the material I have read and encountered on marketing automation, I found Brian's case the most compelling. It actually helped inspire me to write this book, and to learn more about marketing automation myself. One of the simple reasons came down to how he talked about what really matters: that in the end, it allowed him to spend more time with his family.

> This is a short, 2.5 min version that captures the spirit: https://infusionsoft.wistia.com/medias/62oi9vaeeh

> And a longer, 20 min version tells the "whole" story. It requires the purchase of a library of videos from a conference (2015), but it might be worth looking at as you consider investing in marketing automation: http://attendicon.com/agenda/library

Brian Young of Home Painters Toronto discovered that marketing automation had a powerful impact on his business, helping to increase revenue significantly and reduce the time required to manage all the details. In this interview we discuss some of his story.

Todd: What kind of impact do you think marketing automation can bring?

Brian: I think it can free you up to grow your business as big as you want it, and lower your amount of hands on work as much as you want.

How important do you think it is to leverage marketing automation, from a competitive standpoint?

Marketing automation allows you to grow unbelievably fast, working less, more efficient, more profitable. It puts you so far ahead of your competition - they have no way of catching up. It's absolutely essential

You can grow more exponentially in short amount of time. It's amazing quickly you can grow with automation under the right circumstances. The thing about automation is that it forces you to break your business down into bite sized pieces. So for example it forces you to create content for each stage, so it allows you to figure out where problems are. (ex: I'm having a lot of problems at this stage - the potential customer is stuck there, we need to fix it). This kind of evaluation can help you figure out where the issues. Otherwise, you're kind of blind - you're asking yourself -- why do I not have sales?

So what's been the biggest benefit to you from marketing automation? Money or time?

Both. I would say time though; you can always make money. Time is precious, you can't replace it. It's organized our business - we have processes, stages, we've broken it down, so I can delegate parts of my business, so we're maximizing every lead. And we're processing every lead so we can close or nurture them. For example, if we want a lead, we want to put it in a particular stage (ex: "hot leads" or "weak leads") and follow up appropriately depending on what type of client they are.

How did you find out about marketing automation? How long was it before you took action?

I didn't know a thing about it before Infusionsoft; being an old school painter. I hired a business coach Mike Torgerson, and he opened up my world to Infusionsoft, we started a website, got hooked up on Google Adwords. I had declining sales for 15 years - I was at the point where I was desperate, didn't have much choice.

How many employees did you have "before" Infusionsoft, and what were your yearly revenues? What about "after"?

Before Infusionsoft, 6-8 subcontractors - 375k gross revenues. Customer satisfaction rating was 85 percent. No customer database.

After Infusionsoft, 3 years - 1.3 million gross revenue. Customer satisfaction 98 percent. Customer database grew from 200 to 6,000. 8 in-house employees. 25 subcontractors.

Was cashflow tight at the beginning? What convinced you to invest in Infusionsoft?

The good thing was I did have some cashflow - some revenue to work with. It's just that it was going down and I saw the writing on the wall. Experts recommended that I had no choice but to go for marketing automation. I didn't really know what the power was until I got it.

Do you think it's something someone can do "on their own", or do you believe it's best to bring in help?

I think it's ideal if you can bring in help - especially in my case because I knew nothing. With assistance, I learned it in 3 years - on my own it would have taken me 15-20 years! At first I had a really tough time with Infusionsoft, and my business coach referred me to Kelsey Bratcher, and he's the guy who really helped turned my business around; if it wasn't for outside help I wouldn't have had the success I did.

A good resource makes the process go a lot faster. As a business owner you're really good at 1-2 things and average everything else. I was good at sales, maybe running the business -- but terrible at the marketing side. If you have the resources, hire someone.

How do you justify the investment of money and time on bringing in assistance, if you're on a limited budget?

If you have a limited budget, you have to cut corners. You could join Meetup groups, go online, do your research -- there are ways of doing it cheaper. Find people who've done it, beg for information. Self-starter research. For example, go outside your area, if you're in painting - go to a roofer. You don't *have* to have a coach - you can do it on your own if you search.

Even with assistance or guidance from an agency, how much time do you think a person would need to spend in order to realize gains from Infusionsoft?

It was extremely difficult for me because I'm not a tech smart guy - it really depends on your tech ability. If you're pretty good techwise, basics 1-2 months. If you're not good, it might take a bit longer.

For working on getting marketing automation going, and refining and optimizing it, we spent about 350 hours in 3 years, which works out to about 10 hours a month. Even now, I spend 2 hours a week maintaining and testing things. To be clear, we're not just building automation - we're building my business.

Given the adjustment it was, and how you had to build your business, how did you motivate yourself to carry things through?

One of the biggest issues with being an entrepreneur can be being lonely - you're very isolated. That's one of the biggest problems - so just don't get down on yourself. I go to YouTube for inspiration. I love Tony Robbins, and Rocky is one of my inspirations (see the video). It's really tough, going through all the stress, new issues you come up each day. You need people to help you through it.

Definitely use agencies, motivational videos, friends, groups (ex: Meetup in general). You need support or else you'll fail.

Given how hard it is, is it worth it?

Absolutely!

If you're starting from square one, do you think you should first get all the standard digital marketing pieces in place? Or do you think that marketing automation should be planned for from Day One?

It's always better to do marketing automation from day one - if you don't have the budget to hire outside assistance, you can learn it. Any business needs a client base. Without a database, you're dead. Start from Day 1, start in small chunks, at least get basic information in place, a way to collect customer data. Don't think everything has to be perfect - it's an ongoing process, it never stops.

To be realistic, I follow the 80% rule. I don't try to get perfect - try to get 80% of what you want. If your goal is 1 million in a year, don't get too focused on that 1 million, or it may seem insurmountable. Just get started with something, anything, and build it brick by brick.

How did you go about doing research on your customers, in order to get the most out of marketing automation? Is it a matter of figuring out what they need, where they're at in the buying cycle, and sending messages then?

Yeah - the best thing to do is ask the customers. Ex: Did you like this? Were you happy with how fast we responded? Was this good, was that good? And some would say "Too many emails" about one thing, or too *little* emails about another thing. So talk to customers. No one knows your customers better than you do. Talk to them, ask them, get their feedback. We have automated this part of our business via Reputation Loop. Once we are done a job we send out a questionnaire asking for their feedback and how their experience was with us. If we get a 5 out of 5 rating then we encourage them to post the review on our most popular review sites. If we get a negative feedback, then we are quick to be on top of things to fix things fast before things can get out of control.

How did you go about "segmenting" your customers, splitting them into groups so you can give a message tailored to a group?

The thing about segmenting is you start off simple. As you start selling, there's two types: one is ready to buy, one is not ready to buy. In terms of groups, as you start to look at it, you discover that there's some types of customers you want to deal with, and others you don't. You notice that there are customers at different stages: some are ready to buy, some may be ready to buy later. When you can start thinking of your customers in stages (and when you start talking to them), you can figure out what kind of messages people want to hear at each stage. Like if they're "not ready to buy", you can ask them what do they need? An offer for more information? A discount?

We started simple, with six stages. And after testing, refining, and just as importantly, talking to customers, we arrived at 12 stages, which was right for us:

1 New Lead
2 Wants quote
3 Appointment set
4-6 Separate into different customer types: hot leads, weak leads, real weak leads
7 Verbal yes
8 Job booked
9 Job in production
10 Job complete
11 Job paid in full
12 Dead leads

(For more information about the lessons I learned as we integrated marketing automation in my business, visit www.passionatebrian.com)

Were there any surprises, positive or negative, that stick out to you, when you were learning marketing automation?

Positive: I didn't have to do everything myself anymore!

Another great aha: I could hire someone to do these processes. It allowed me to delegate, whereas before I had to do it myself.

- Aha: With marketing automation, I could measure what's going on, hourly, weekly, monthly, so I could have a better sense of performance than I had before.
- Aha: With things more automated, I could manage my business from anywhere in the world.
- Aha: Implementing better systems allows me to be more organized and keep in touch with my customers, which is really important to me.

Negative: I learned the lesson that if you aren't careful you can turn off your customers. This happened a couple of times and I tweaked it. But this is important -- talking to people is what allowed me to fix it and improve it. Make sure you don't get too far away from your business. Sometimes you have to be really careful not to spam people. You want to be really strategic. Be careful about letting other people do your content, because you know your customers better than anyone. You want to be editing all content, to make sure it's coming from you.

Is there any particular technique or "trick" that stands out to you, that you'd be willing to share, that you learned?

TIP: Don't get too wrapped up in money goals. Start to break the business into chunks, get it outside of your head and down on paper. Think about your customers, talk to them, think about the specific buying stages they are in, and how to talk to them in each of these specific stages, then nurture them from one stage to another. If you think too abstractly, you'll get bogged down. Just take it step by step. Think about it - for us it was a 350 hour effort over three years - but the car doesn't drive itself. It's had a huge impact, on revenue, everything else. I still spend 2 hours a week on it. But it's absolutely worth it.

--

NOTE FROM THE AUTHOR: Of all the material I have read and encountered on marketing automation, I found Brian's case the most compelling. It actually helped inspire me to write this book, and to learn more about marketing automation myself. One of the simple reasons came down to how he talked about what really matters: that in the end, it allowed him to spend more time with his family.

> This is a short, 2.5 min version that captures the spirit: https://infusionsoft.wistia.com/medias/62oi9vaeeh

> And a longer, 20 min version tells the "whole" story. It requires the purchase of a library of videos from a conference (2015), but it might be worth looking at as you consider investing in marketing automation: http://attendicon.com/agenda/library

Conclusion/Discussion

Congratulations on soaking in a case study! Motivation is really important, and I think it's good to have a realistic look at the pros and cons, the challenges and the benefits. The bottom line is that Brian's case study shows that with the right commitment, the right investment of time and resources, you can make things happen that can have a significant impact on your business. And my favorite part of it is – the possibility of spending more time with your family.

If you're ready to take things to the next level, you're also welcome to schedule a free consultation, to see how Rainmaker Internet Marketing can help your business make use of marketing automation. Please visit rainma.com/automation

For More Information

For a complete list of links and resources, visit <u>rainma.com/book</u>

Printed in Great Britain
by Amazon